D1340038

Securing
the Cloud

Security Strategies for the
Ubiquitous Data Center

Securing the Cloud

Security Strategies for the Ubiquitous Data Center

Curtis Franklin, Jr.
Brian J. S. Chee

CRC Press
Taylor & Francis Group
Boca Raton London New York

CRC Press is an imprint of the
Taylor & Francis Group, an **informa** business

AN AUERBACH BOOK

CRC Press
Taylor & Francis Group
6000 Broken Sound Parkway NW, Suite 300
Boca Raton, FL 33487-2742

First issued in paperback 2022

© 2019 by Taylor & Francis Group, LLC
CRC Press is an imprint of Taylor & Francis Group, an Informa business

No claim to original U.S. Government works

ISBN 13: 978-1-03-247571-4 (pbk)
ISBN 13: 978-1-4665-6920-1 (hbk)

This book contains information obtained from authentic and highly regarded sources. Reasonable efforts have been made to publish reliable data and information, but the author and publisher cannot assume responsibility for the validity of all materials or the consequences of their use. The authors and publishers have attempted to trace the copyright holders of all material reproduced in this publication and apologize to copyright holders if permission to publish in this form has not been obtained. If any copyright material has not been acknowledged please write and let us know so we may rectify in any future reprint.

Except as permitted under U.S. Copyright Law, no part of this book may be reprinted, reproduced, transmitted, or utilized in any form by any electronic, mechanical, or other means, now known or hereafter invented, including photocopying, microfilming, and recording, or in any information storage or retrieval system, without written permission from the publishers.

For permission to photocopy or use material electronically from this work, please access www.copyright. com (http://www.copyright.com/) or contact the Copyright Clearance Center, Inc. (CCC), 222 Rosewood Drive, Danvers, MA 01923, 978-750-8400. CCC is a not-for-profit organization that provides licenses and registration for a variety of users. For organizations that have been granted a photocopy license by the CCC, a separate system of payment has been arranged.

Trademark Notice: Product or corporate names may be trademarks or registered trademarks, and are used only for identification and explanation without intent to infringe.

Publisher's Note
The publisher has gone to great lengths to ensure the quality of this reprint but points out that some imperfections in the original copies may be apparent.

Visit the Taylor & Francis Web site at
http://www.taylorandfrancis.com

and the CRC Press Web site at
http://www.crcpress.com

Trademarks Covered in This Book

Active Directory®, Azure®, Excel®, Exchange®, Hyper-V®, Lync®, Microsoft®, Microsoft Dynamics®, Microsoft Exchange Server®, Microsoft® RemoteFX®, Office®, Office 365®, OneDrive®, SharePoint®, Skype®, Skype for Business, SQL Server®, System Center Virtual Machine Manager®, Windows®, Windows NT® Server 4.0, Windows® 7, Windows® 8, Windows® Desktop, Windows Server®, Windows Server® 2000, Windows Server® 2008, Windows Server® 2012, Windows Server® 2012 R2, Windows Server® 2016, Windows® Vista™, and Windows® XP are trademarks and/or registered trademarks of Microsoft Corporation.

Alexa™, Amazon Elastic Block Store™, EBS™, Amazon Elastic Compute Cloud™, Amazon EC2™, Amazon Glacier™, Amazon Simple Notification Service™, SNS™, Amazon SQS™, Amazon Web Services™, AWS™, and DynamoDB™ are trademarks of Amazon.com, Inc.

Apache® Hadoop® is a trademark of The Apache Software Foundation in the United States and/or other countries. No endorsement by The Apache Software Foundation is implied by the use of these marks.

Apple®, iPad®, iPhone®, FaceTime®, Mac®, Mac OS®, Apple® OS X®, OS X® Server, and Siri® are registered trademarks of Apple, Inc., in the United States and other countries.

ArcGIS® is a registered trademark of Environmental Systems Research Institute, Inc. (ESRI).

AutoCAD®, AutoDesk® Revit®, and Maya® are registered trademarks of Autodesk, Inc., and/or its subsidiaries and/or affiliates, in the United States.

Avocent® DSView™ is a trademark of the Avocent Corporation.

Barbican®, Ceilometer®, Cinder®, Designate®, Glance®, Heat®, Horizon®, Ironic®, Keystone®, Manila®, Mistral®, Neutron®, Nova®, OpenStack®, Sahara®, Searchlight,® Swift®, Trove®, and Zaqar® are registered trademarks of the OpenStack Foundation.

Black Hat® is a registered trademark of UBM LLC.

BLAST® is a registered trademark of the National Library of Medicine.

Box® is a registered trademark of Box, Inc.

CenturyLink® is a trademark of CenturyLink, Inc.

Chromebooks™, Chromeboxes™, Google®, Google Apps™, Google Docs™, Google Drive™, Google Glass™, Google Maps™, Google Translate™, and Google Hangouts™ are trademarks of Google LLC.

Cisco®, IOS®, and Jabber® are registered trademark of Cisco Systems, Inc. and/or its affiliates in the United States and certain other countries.

Citrix®, Citrix® NetScaler®, MetaFrame®, WinFrame®, XenApp®, XenDesktop®, and XenServer® are registered trademarks of Citrix Systems, Inc.

CNN® is a registered trademark of CABLE NEWS NETWORK, INC.

DB2®, IBM®, and IBM® PowerVM® are registered trademarks of the International Business Machines Corporation in the United States, other countries, or both.

Dell™ and Wyse™ are trademarks of Dell Inc. or its subsidiaries.

Dragon® Dictate is a registered trademark of Nuance Communications, Inc.

Dropbox® is a registered trademark of Dropbox, Inc.

Drupal® is a registered trademark of Dries Buytaert.

eBay® is a registered trademark of eBay, Inc., in the United States and internationally.

Facebook™ Messenger is a trademark of Facebook, Inc.

FlexLM™ and FlexPublisher™ are trademarks of Globetrotter, Inc.

HP® is a registered trademark of Hewlett-Packard Company.

Intel® and Intel® Xeon® is a registered trademark of Intel Corporation or its subsidiaries in the United States and/or other countries.

Interop™ is a trademark of Interop Technologies.

IxChariot® is a registered trademark of Ixia in the United States and other countries.

Java® and Oracle® are registered trademarks of Oracle Corporation.

Joomla!® is a registered trademark of Open Source Matters, Inc., in the United States and other countries.

Kool-Aid® is a registered trademark of Perkins Products Company.

LinkedIn® is a registered trademark of LinkedIn Corporation.

Linux® is the registered trademark of Linus Torvalds in the United States and other countries.

LoadRunner® is a registered trademark of Mercury Interactive.

Maserati® is a trademark of OFFICINE ALFIERI MASERATI S.P.A.

Mathematica® is a registered trademark of Wolfram Research, Inc.

MATLAB® is a registered trademark of The MathWorks, Inc.

Mini Maxwell™ is a trademark and InterWorking Labs® and KMAX® are registered trademarks of InterWorking Labs, Inc.

Nirvanix® is a registered trademark of Nirvanix Inc.

OpenFlow® is a registered trademark of the Open Networking Foundation.

Post-It® is a registered trademark of the 3M Company.

Rackspace® is a registered trademark of Rackspace US, Inc., in the United States and/or other countries.

Raritan® CommandCenter® is a registered trademark of Raritan, Inc.

Raspberry Pi® is a registered trademark of the Raspberry Pi Foundation.

Red Hat®, Red Hat® KVM, and Red Hat® QEMU are registered trademarks of Red Hat, Inc. in the United States and other countries.

Renderman® is a trademark of PIXAR.

ScienceLogic EM7™ is a trademark of ScienceLogic, Inc.

Slashdot Media® is a registered trademark of SourceForge in the United States and in other countries.

SonicWall® is a registered trademark of SonicWALL, Inc.

SONY® is a registered trademark of Sony Corporation.

SplashID™ Key Safe is a trademark of SplashData, Inc.

StealthWatch® and Lancope® are registered trademarks of Lancope, Inc.

Sunny Boy® and Sunny WebBox® are registered trademarks of SMA Solar Technology AG.

SunSpec® is a registered trademark of SunSpec Alliance, Inc.

Symmetricom® NTP Server is a registered trademark of Symmetricom, Inc.

Target® is a registered trademark of Target Brands, Inc.

Tetris® is a registered trademark of the Tetris Holding Company and is licensed to The Tetris Company, LLC.

The Home Depot® is a registered trademark of Home Depot Product Authority, LLC.

UNIVAC® is a registered trademark of Eckert-Mauchly Computer Corporation (EMCC).

Unix® is a registered trademark in the United States and other countries, licensed exclusively through X/Open Company Ltd.

VMware®, WMware ESX®, VMware vCloud Director®, and VMware VSphere® Storage Appliance™ (VSA) are trademarks of VMware, Inc., in the United States and/or other jurisdictions.

WebLOAD™ is a trademark of RadView™ Software Ltd.

What'sUp® Gold is a registered trademark of Ipswitch, Inc.

Wikipedia® is a registered trademark of Wikimedia Foundation.

WinRunner® is a registered trademark of Memory Interactive.

WordPress® is a registered trademark of WordPress Foundation.

Dedication

To the InteropNET NOC team, InteropNET Volunteers (ITMs), and the volunteer coordinators (who herded the cats). Thanks to the team that was integral to the process of ensuring that the interoperating dreams of the original Internet designers actually interoperated. You made a difference.

Contents

Preface

As we write this book, the concept of cloud computing has entered the mainstream, although not all organizations have chosen to dive in. Thousands of IT professionals, enterprise executives, consultants, students, and generally curious, intelligent people have been left wondering whether "The Cloud" can be part of their computing world. One of the most frequently asked set of questions revolves around just how secure their important data can be if it's stored in something as nebulous sounding as a cloud. It is for all these curious people that we wrote this book.

Acknowledgments

We would like to thank Karl Auerbach, Joel Snyder, Daniel Stewart, and Tom Cross for sharing their unvarnished opinions with us, as well as, of course, our wives, Carol and Kathy, who put up with us writing this book for far too long.

We would also like to thank our editor/typesetter, Marje Pollack (DerryField Publishing Services), who should have shot us long ago.

About the Authors

Curtis Franklin, Jr., is Senior Editor at *Dark Reading*. In addition, he works on audio and video programming for *Dark Reading* and contributes to activities at Interop™ ITX, Black Hat®, and other conferences. Curtis is also a co-host for the popular *This Week in Enterprise Tech* podcast.

Curtis has been writing about technologies and products in computing and networking since the early 1980s. He has contributed to or been on staff at a number of technology-industry publications, including *Information Week, Light Reading, Enterprise Efficiency, ChannelWeb, Network Computing, InfoWorld, PCWorld, Dark Reading, Circuit Cellar INK, BYTE,* and *ITWorld.com,* on subjects ranging from mobile enterprise computing to enterprise security and wireless networking.

Curtis is the author of thousands of articles, the co-author of five books, and has been a frequent speaker at computer and networking industry conferences across North America and Europe. His most popular previous book, *The Absolute Beginner's Guide to Podcasting*, with co-author George Colombo, was published by Que Books (October 2005). His most recent book, *Cloud Computing: Technologies and Strategies of the Ubiquitous Data Center*, with co-author Brian Chee, was published by the Taylor & Francis Group and released in April 2010.

When he's not writing, Curtis is a painter, photographer, cook, and multi-instrumentalist musician. He is active in amateur radio (KG4GWA), running, and stand-up paddleboarding, and he is a certified Florida Master Naturalist.

Brian J. S. Chee lives in Kaneohe, Hawaii, with his family tracing back four generations in Hawaii. An admitted generalist, starting with building IMSAI 8080s, writing assembler on punch cards for IBM 360s, and jumping into becoming one of the first 10 Novell Instructors outside of Novell, Inc. It was with the GSA Office of Information Security that he traveled the world working on secure data/video/voice communications systems for just about every three-letter agency in the book. Now, working as a researcher at the University of Hawaii School of Ocean and Earth Science and Technology (www.soest.hawaii.edu), he has gotten to work on underwater cabled observatories, autonomous underwater vehicles, SWATH ships, deep dive submarines and ROVs, volcanic sensors, and emerging energy systems. His greatest job was working with InteropNET NOC, where he became part of a team that has affected the majority of the standards of the Internet while creating methodologies for the interoperability of Internet communications systems.

Look for his publications at *InfoWorld* and podcasts for *This Week in Enterprise Technology* on the TWiT.tv network, as well as the aforementioned first book in this series, *Cloud Computing: Technologies and Strategies of the Ubiquitous Data Center.*

Chapter 1

Introduction

Why This Book Is Needed

When we began writing *Cloud Computing: Technologies and Strategies of the Ubiquitous Data Center*[1] in 2008, the idea that an enterprise would entrust its data and operations to a computing platform on which function was divorced from specific hardware or geography was on the cutting edge of enterprise information technology. As we write this book, the concept of cloud computing has entered the mainstream, although not all organizations have chosen to dive in. Thousands of IT professionals, enterprise executives, consultants, students, and generally curious, intelligent people have been left wondering whether "The Cloud" can be part of their computing world. One of the most frequently asked set of questions in the wondering process revolves around just how secure their important data can be if it's stored in something as nebulous sounding as a cloud. It is for all these curious people that we wrote this book.

Perhaps you're an IT executive who has been working in the field for a number of years. You have a reasonably good idea of how security works in the traditional data center, and you've begun to wrap your head around the particulars of security as it's applied to virtual servers and storage

1

appliances. When it comes to the cloud, though, you heard early on that security was a problem and you haven't really been able to dive into the subject deeply enough to decide whether that impression is correct or just convenient. Now, your users and the rest of the management team is bringing up the cloud every time an IT problem is mentioned. You've decided that you need to get a handle on just how secure your data would be in the cloud, but you don't know where to start.

We wrote this book for you.

Maybe you're part of the management team at a small company. Or perhaps you're the entire management team at a small company. You're not a computer expert, but the responsibility for making the final computer decisions rests on your shoulders, and people, from vendors to consultants to your own employees, keep bringing up the cloud. You've heard horror stories about how vulnerable things can be when they're stored "out there," but the economics sure are enticing. You'd love to be able to have a solid discussion with cloud providers and IT people without feeling like they're speaking some horrible language that you don't understand. You need a primer on the concepts behind security and the cloud and a guide book to this cloudy land—something that can help you understand where your data can have a good time and which places you should avoid at all costs.

We wrote this book for you.

It could be that you're a consultant who's built a solid business helping companies with their computer issues. Your command of the classic client and server model is solid, you've helped firms move their applications to the Web, and you've even figured out how to make virtualization work for some of your larger customers. Now, you believe that there's a business model that would be viable for you and your clients if you could help them see how cloud computing might work for their situation. First, though, you have to be able to show them that their information will be safe if they store it in a cloud architecture that's been portrayed as the IT version of the "Wild, Wild West." You need to make sure that you understand the concepts and can describe them to customers in simple, direct language.

We wrote this book for you.

You could be a student working in a class on security or cloud architecture. It's possible you're a student who hasn't been assigned this book for a class, but you're interested in the cloud and security because you've heard that it's important and you want to be able to find a job after you graduate from university. You're pretty good with basic programming, and you're rapidly building your knowledge of different facets of information processing and general computing. You might even have decided that becoming an expert in cloud computing could be a good direction for the early stages of your career. Before you can move from the academic to the real world, however, you have to be able to talk intelligently about how cloud computing can reasonably be used for companies that are doing real work "out there." You need to understand the basics and have a real foundation in the theory so you can start building a practice that makes sense.

We wrote this book for you.

And it might just be that you're none of the above. You're interested in cloud computing because you keep reading about how it's the greatest thing since sliced bread, and you're interested in security because you keep reading about massive data breaches, the impact of cyber-warfare, and the scary consequences of identity theft and you want to know how companies are able to keep anything safe and private when it's stored in something as open sounding as "The Cloud." When you're interested in something you read about it, whether we're talking about cloud security or the impact of the Crimean War on 20th-century European politics.

We even wrote this book for you.

A reasonable person could reasonably ask how we intend to make one book meet the needs of all these different people. The answer is that we take the position that everyone reading this book is smart and curious. Everyone reading this book has some basic knowledge about computers and networks. And everyone reading this book deserves to have the information laid out in terms that use jargon as little as possible and build on basic concepts until we've conveyed what you need to know about security of, by, and for the cloud. Now, it's also important for you to understand what this book won't do for you.

If you're looking for a book that contains a lot of programming examples and configuration files that can be copied into routers and firewalls, then you really should expand your search. If you're looking for a book that prepares you for a particular certification exam, with specific answers and practice exams, then there are other titles that will better suit your needs. If, on the other hand, you'd like to know what some of the leading experts in the field think about the current state of cloud computing security and its likely future; if you're looking for something that will let you hold your own in a discussion of cloud computing security; or if you want to be able to fine-tune the level of your nonsense detector when people are coming at you with cloud security claims, then sit back, settle in, and grab your favorite beverage. It's time to get started on the book that is absolutely the right one for you.

Companies and organizations care so deeply about cloud security because they are adopting the cloud in large and growing numbers. What kind of numbers? According to a report by Cisco®,[2] by 2014, more than half of all data loads (and in this case we're talking about business information processing) will be processed in cloud computing centers, and only a minority will be processed in traditional data centers. If companies are going to move a growing percentage of their processing to a cloud computing architecture, it makes sense that their interest in securing the data that lives outside their traditional data center would increase apace.

Among the reasons given for a reluctance to go to the cloud, security concerns frequently top the list. As cloud deployments have expanded, cloud storage and applications have become part of infrastructures that fall under regulatory control, leading many IT professionals to wonder how, or if, the cloud can be considered sufficiently secure to meet regulatory compliance muster. If cloud computing were still experimental rather than a part of mainstream enterprise IT, this reticence would have little overall impact. As it is, though, individuals who have an incomplete or mistaken understanding of the security issues within cloud computing may find themselves placing their organizations at a competitive disadvantage because of a reluctance to embrace a computing model that could have significant advantages in their business situation.

Cloud computing is moving out of experimental and niche deployments to play a significant role in the everyday run-of-business IT infrastructure of a growing number of mainstream businesses.

From another perspective, advances in cloud applications have led to a growing number of businesses that are eager to use cloud capabilities as part of their security infrastructure, protecting both data center and mobile platforms from their remote point of view.

This book takes the position that cloud security is an extension of recognized, established security principles into cloud-based deployments. Exploring how those principles can be put into practice in protecting the cloud, protecting the traditional infrastructure from the cloud, or a hybrid of the two is what we intend to do in the remainder of this book.

In times of rapid change, both of the organization and its customers/partners/suppliers, the ability to rapidly change the scale and capability of the IT infrastructure is critical to success. Cloud computing is, in many ways, perfect for the times in which business now finds itself.

Flexibility is inherent in the cloud model of computing. Computing resources, whether processor cycles or storage capacity, are treated as nearly infinitely flexible commodities, deployed or released as demand requires. This is perfect for matching IT services to the needs of the business and is unlikely to be supplanted as a model until something even more flexible replaces it.

Unfortunately, cloud computing is evolving so rapidly that regulations and security technology have not necessarily been able to keep pace. This means that IT professionals are frequently left to force fit pre-existing models and technologies onto new infrastructures and architectures for which they may be very poor fits, indeed. This book will look at the way those "square peg/round hole" matings are being implemented and suggest ways in which the pegs, the holes, or both may be adjusted for a more perfect fit.

One of the important reasons for this book is that the area covered by the word "cloud" has increased significantly in the last five years. Where cloud computing once meant straightforward services obtained under contract from a public cloud provider, there are now clouds that incorporate a wide variety of services and applications—services that may be hosted on a public cloud infrastructure, on a company's own servers, or on a combination of both types of servers.

Public cloud services are still what most people mean when they speak of the cloud, and they remain the focal point of security efforts. Quite a bit of this focus comes from the simple fact that vital enterprise data is stored or processed on systems owned by another company—systems that are accessed via the Internet. Knowing what is possible in protecting cloud-stored data is critical, but by itself, it misses a major facet of cloud security. A cloud architecture allows for a view from outside the protected data and processing infrastructure. This protection from "the high ground" is, in many ways, consistent with traditional military strategy. Although the analogy to physical defense can be stretched only so far without breaking, there are elements that provide a useful illustration of critical points, as you'll see a bit later in the book.

Public, Private, and Hybrid Clouds

One of the reasons that analogies to the physical world run into trouble in the realm of cloud computing is that The Cloud (as if such a unified, single entity truly existed) doesn't really lend itself to neat categories. There is the public cloud mentioned in the last section. There are private clouds, in which the operational characteristics of public clouds—on-demand, elastic, self-provisioned computing services and storage—are applied to computing and storage infrastructures owned by (or contracted for on an exclusive basis with a service provider) the enterprise customer. To see what the differences are in a simplified format, see Figure 1.1.

From a security standpoint, these private clouds have as much in common with traditional computing infrastructures as they do with public clouds, a situation that provides its own set of complications. Then there are the hybrid clouds, in which the entire computing structure is made up from pieces of private clouds, pieces of public clouds, and pieces of traditional computing infrastructure all brought together in a whirring IT blender.

These hybrid clouds can be as complex as the description suggests, and protecting them can be equally complicated. You'll see in the Table of Contents that we discuss hybrid clouds and their protection in great detail.

What This Book Will Cover

Security in the cloud is a wide-ranging topic that requires basic knowledge in a number of areas and deeper knowledge in several others. This book will guide you from an introduction to general IT security through the basics of cloud architectures, with the goal of helping you understand how security applies to the various sorts of clouds—and how various clouds can be applied to the problems of security in many different circumstances.

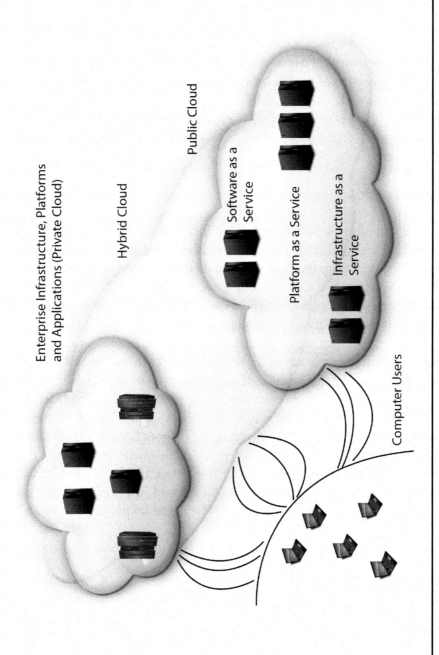

Enterprise Infrastructure, Platforms and Applications (Private Cloud)

Hybrid Cloud

Public Cloud

Software as a Service

Platform as a Service

Infrastructure as a Service

Computer Users

Figure 1.1. Public, private, and hybrid clouds are similar in structure and architecture, but distinct in ownership.

Security Basics

We begin with security in IT and how it has evolved to the understanding that it must be viewed as a 360-degree issue if it's to be effective. Part of this introduction, understandably, is a discussion of precisely what "360-degree security" means and why it's so important. This point will be critical in latter parts of the book when we discuss just how security can be by and of the cloud. This foundation, therefore, isn't just a way to increase the number of pages to make you feel the book's purchase price is justified; it's necessary if we're to effectively convey an understanding of the topic.

Cloud Basics

Once we complete our discussion of security basics, we turn to the other part of our foundation: a discussion of the cloud. On the one hand, defining a simple term like "cloud computing" and giving examples of its applications seems like a simple task as seen in Figure 1.2. On the other hand, we're working in a world that has seen the phrase "cloud computing" applied to a wide variety of technologies and products. When those products and technologies are combined in the many different permutations possible, then it becomes necessary to look at the term and what it means.

In the second major section of this book, we present the different pieces of the overall information processing puzzle covered by different types of clouds—from Infrastructure as a Service (IaaS) through Software as a Service (SaaS)—as well as cloud storage through on-demand cloud processing in public, private, and hybrid deployment models. By the time you've gone through this section, you'll have the foundation necessary to begin applying the security basics learned in the first section to the cloud to protect the cloud, or use the cloud to protect traditional enterprise infrastructure.

Protection by the Cloud

Why, you might well ask, would we begin looking at protection by the cloud rather than protection of the cloud? Isn't the cloud an inherently risky proposition that must have layer upon layer of security imposed

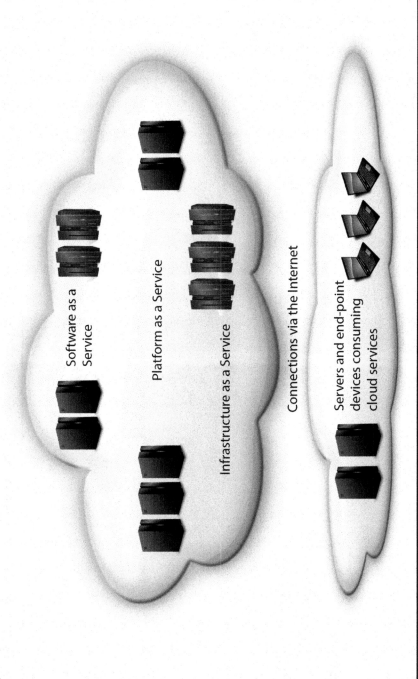

Software as a
Service

Platform as a Service

Infrastructure as a Service

Connections via the Internet

Servers and end-point
devices consuming
cloud services

Figure 1.2. Cloud computing is computing function abstracted as services available in an elastic, on–demand fashion.

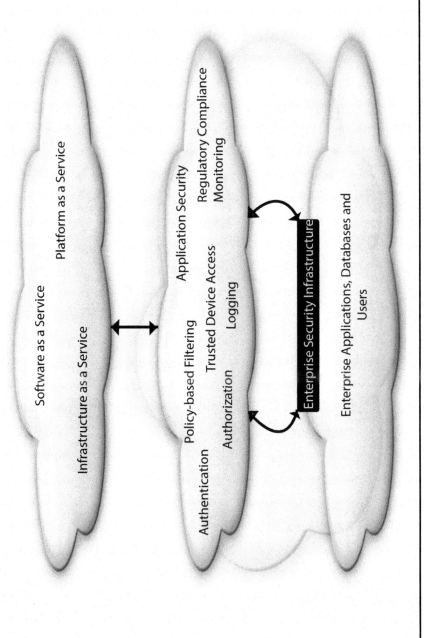

Figure 1.3. Security from the cloud can protect cloud computing and traditional IT functions and users.

upon it? If you've read the previous sections (rather than being one of those people who skips ahead to the good stuff), then you know that the cloud is no more inherently risky than any other form of computing. To the contrary, this section will teach you that clouds can be valuable assets when protecting traditional IT components, other cloud components, or systems made up from combinations of the two types in a model shown in Figure 1.3.

We begin by examining the sort of protection with which most people are familiar: perimeter protection. The concept is as simple and direct as the classic walled city. You build something impregnable and dare the marauding forces to come through the wall to lay hands on the jewels at the heart of the operation. The trouble with the traditional model is that the defense of the wall (and what it protects) has to be accomplished from inside the walls. When protection can come from the cloud, however, it can have the advantage of detecting and stopping intrusion attempts before they reach the ramparts.

The jewels at the heart of the operation are the databases and other repositories of information that form the center of the modern enterprise. Cloud-based security options for protecting the contents of the network can provide protection to the data both "at rest"—while it is stored in the enterprise databases—and "in motion"—as it travels between storage and application, or between components of the application infrastructure, as shown in Figure 1.3. Properly designed and configured cloud-based protection for enterprise data can allow information to be securely stored and processed at the most efficient and effective location while maintaining the integrity of the data and the privacy of customers, patients, or employees.

As computing architectures become more complex, the advantages of security imposed from outside the data center become more compelling. This is particularly true when the architecture of the compute environment includes virtual and cloud computing elements. These are different computing architectures, but they share a number of characteristics that make them challenging to secure with traditional tools and methods. (For details on the difference, we urge you to run out now to buy our first book, *Cloud Computing: Technologies and Strategies of the Ubiquitous Data Center.*[3])

One of the primary challenging characteristics is the ephemeral nature of virtual servers, networks, and clients. When local security is chasing after these virtual devices, which can be created and torn down in rapid-fire fashion across many different hardware platforms, the chasing process can get in the way of security. When the security can be abstracted from the computing environment to be protected, though, several levels of frantic, unnecessary effort can be avoided. We'll look at just why this is so, and how the transcendent calm of cloud-based security can be effective, in a later section. It's important to realize, though, that in addition to protecting the traditional data center (and its virtualized successor), cloud security can be quite useful in protecting the cloud itself.

Protection of the Cloud

One of the frequently cited arguments against cloud computing is that the cloud is an inherently insecure place for data.[4] It's true that there have been a handful of notable lapses in security from public cloud providers in the recent past.[5] It's also true that the nature of cloud computing can make defending the cloud with the services of a traditional security infrastructure a challenging proposition. Fortunately, there are other truths that make these two notable facts a bit easier to cope with when looked at through the IT administrator's lens.

The first convenient truth is that not all clouds are public clouds. This is the point that seems simplest and yet is often overlooked (or ignored) by cloud computing's detractors. Trying to provide enterprise-class protection to data parked in Google Docs™ or DropBox® is one thing; applying enterprise security to a private cloud (whether owned by the organization or contracted through a service provider) is something else entirely. Protecting data stored in public cloud offerings is largely a matter of policy enforcement, though there are appliance-based options that can be very useful when making sure that employees and contractors comply with regulatory requirements.

A cloud facility that is private (either through ownership or contract) is much more relatable to traditional security, even though certain concepts (and a number of tactics) must be revisited in order to ensure success. This book will examine both strategic and tactical implications of cloud protection and will help you understand why either hybrid or fully cloud-based security implementations can be used to great effect in securing the cloud.

And that brings us to the next convenient truth: The nature of cloud computing makes cloud-based security a realistic choice for robust security of cloud-hosted data and processes. The concepts of hybrid clouds and hybrid security infrastructures, in which elements of traditional centralized security and cloud-based security are used in concert to protect data and processes that span traditional and cloud-based data and processing, can become complex, but the later chapters in this book will look at the individual components and how they can be used together for effective security. We will also examine just how to evaluate scenarios in which it may be best to reject hybrid security solutions in favor of simpler approaches that might be more appropriate and more effective. In the end, though, the goal of this book is to help administrators understand the conditions and situations in which cloud security—protecting either traditional IT infrastructures, cloud computing infrastructures, or both—can be superior to classic data security.

Why the Cloud Is Superior Security

An understanding of the benefits (and costs) of cloud security will necessarily include an understanding of the threats against which data and systems must be protected. Anyone reading this book should be clear on a critical point: If we understand IT security in light of the threats of 1995, then the security of 1996 is quite sufficient. The first decades of the 21st century, however, have seen the rise of advanced persistent threats (APTs), state-sponsored malware, shape-shifting adaptive viruses, and other security threats that go far beyond the rather straightforward attacks of previous years. Given the changing threat landscape, cloud computing offers three characteristics that can be critical for different individuals and organizations seeking to make their environment more secure.

The first characteristic is location, or lack of location. Cloud computing platforms offer an external platform from which to secure traditional computing infrastructures and an advantageous position from which to secure other cloud computing assets. This location-based characteristic is crucial for those who want to use cloud computing for security, and an important enabling factor for those seeking to secure computing assets in the cloud.

The second important characteristic is flexibility. Just as on-demand automated provisioning is a defining characteristic of cloud computing, capacity matching and active threat response are characteristics of cloud-based security. Because cloud security is delivered as a service, customers are relieved of requirements to purchase additional hardware in order to meet unexpected increases in demand, to dispose of hardware if demand falls, or to keep the platforms from which security is delivered updated and properly configured. All of this makes cloud security attractive to many customers as it feeds into the third significant characteristic.

Expertise in security is expensive to obtain and difficult to maintain. Realistically, organizations must be able to afford an IT staff of a reasonably large size (often, more than a dozen professionals) before they can afford to dedicate one of those staff positions to security. The ability to devote a security position to cloud security requires an even larger staff. When security services are obtained through a cloud security provider, expertise on the part of the supporting staff is implied, and expertise in the application of the cloud security is frequently available. "Renting" security expertise on this basis can be an affordable and attractive option for many organizations that need to secure either traditional or cloud-based computing assets.

This, then, is what you'll be reading about for the next couple of hundred pages. Security of, by, and for the cloud is neither a universal panacea nor an impossible dream. Let's begin our study by looking at some of the basics of security as they exist in this, the new millennium.

References

1. Chee, Brian J. S. and Franklin, Curtis, Jr. (2010). *Cloud Computing: Technologies and Strategies of the Ubiquitous Data Center,* 1st Edition. Boca Raton, FL: CRC Press.
2. Cisco Systems, Inc. (2011). "Cisco Global Cloud Index: Forecast and Methodology, 2010–2015." Retrieved from http://www.cisco.com/en/US/solutions/collateral/ns341/ns525/ns537/ns705/ns1175/Cloud_Index_White_Paper.pdf
3. Chee, Brian J. S. and Franklin, Curtis, Jr. (2010). *Cloud Computing: Technologies and Strategies of the Ubiquitous Data Center,* 1st Edition. Boca Raton, FL: CRC Press.
4. Schluting, C. (2010). "Sorting Out the Many Faces of Cloud Computing." internet. com. Retrieved from http://www.internet.com/IT/NetworkingAndCommunications/VirtualInfrastructure/Article/42644
5. Tea, K. (2012, Jan. 16). "Can the Cloud Survive More Security Breaches in 2012?" *Business Computing World.* Retrieved from http://www.businesscomputingworld.co.uk/can-the-cloud-survive-more-security-breaches-in-2012/

Chapter 2

We Need a New Model for Security

Security is much more than just good passwords: It's about *defense in depth* and security layered in manageable pieces so that no one person is able to bypass every layer (http://en.wikipedia.org/wiki/Layered_security). What makes cloud security different is that multiple organizations must now become involved. Whether they're internal or external to the security customer doesn't make a difference. It's all about striking a balance between the responsible organizations and managing risk for the entire enterprise.

The authors have a favorite security saying: "Nothing is more secure than an airgap." That's exactly what a lot of Department of Defense (DoD) and other highly secure shops do. They literally do **not** allow any access from the outside world. This means that they're relying upon physical security as their outermost layer. If you're dealing with nuclear launch codes, then the world is certainly hoping for a large dose of paranoia in your security design. However, if you're protecting your daughter's diary and your personal collection of MP3s, then maybe you can loosen up a bit. If the data in question is confidential enterprise information (and especially if it is personal information from customers, patients, or employees) then the proper security level is going to be somewhere between these two extremes. Balancing risk with convenience is the name of the game.

Depending on your industry, various organizations will provide rules for the game and mandates regarding the level of paranoia your organization needs to exercise. However, no one in their right mind would stop with the minimum requirements: Keycards have PINs and/or challenge codes, passwords require a smart card, and perhaps logins require biometrics. There are countless ways to take the technology and practice of security beyond the minimum.

Another favorite saying of the authors is that security should be 90% policy. Anyone who starts a conversation on security with, "I just installed this cool new network security system . . ." is missing the point. Technology without policy is like a freeway without road rules. Someone will inevitably misinterpret what they should be doing and blindly merge into oncoming traffic, with the IT crew left doing the cleanup. Everyone needs to be marching to the beat of the same policy drum.

Policies and Layers

To get computer users moving in the same direction, there are regulations from various agencies in the United States and abroad to provide helpful maps of varying levels of detail. Unfortunately, many of these regulations haven't caught up with technology, and, thus, some of the rules don't apply very well to something as new as cloud computing. For an example, let us look at FISMA.

The US Federal Government regulation on protecting private information is called the Federal Information Security Management Act of 2002 (FISMA). FISMA requirements do not prevent agencies from storing data or using applications in the cloud. In fact, for some time a government "cloud first" policy has encouraged agencies to use clouds as a means to reduce costs. FISMA lays out rules, developed by the National Institute for Science and Technology (NIST) for protecting information. To help both agencies and the cloud providers in serving their needs, the government established the Federal Risk and Authorization Management Program (FedRAMP), a government-wide program that provides a standardized approach to security assessment, authorization, and monitoring cloud products and services.

Another very widespread security map doesn't come from the government but rather from the credit card community. The Payment Card Industry Data Security Standard (PCI DSS) (http://en.wikipedia.org/

wiki/Payment_Card_Industry_Data_Security_Standard) is a standard that delineates what the payment industry considers acceptable risks for connecting systems that process credit cards to public data networks. Although not as aggressively paranoid as FISMA, PCI DSS does require that organizations make sure that they're not using software that has already been broken (i.e., older versions of the Apache web server, which have known vulnerabilities in them) or systems that are incapable of being adequately secured against break-ins.

The key to cloud security is moving away from dependency on location-based security (CICS locked to certain terminals, Media Access Control [MAC], address limitations, etc.) and moving to a system that will allow you to apply your policies in a location-aware, but not location-dependent, manner. We're also *very* firm believers in defense in depth, where security doesn't rely on a single technology or methodology but rather on a system of overlapping technologies and methodologies that strengthen each other (http://www.nsa.gov/ia/_files/support/defenseindepth.pdf) and back one another up in case of a single point of failure.

Location-Independent Security

Although "security" in the information technology world most often is used to describe technology (biometrics, multifactor authentication, etc.) it should, as we've said, bring to mind policies and trust relationships. The Sarbanes-Oxley Act of 2002 (commonly shortened to Sarbox or SOX) has been bashed over and over again by the information technology (IT) world because there isn't anything in the act that describes either how to implement its requirements or audit compliance with those requirements. Although we, too, would wish for more details, we should point out that Sarbanes-Oxley is a set of policies and goals that describe how corporate information should be protected and made available for audits, with just a tiny bit about delegation of authority.

The same thing goes for the Family Educational Rights and Privacy Act (FERPA), which governs educational institutions; the Health Insurance Portability and Accountability Act (HIPAA), which rules the IT and record-keeping activities of hospitals, health-care providers, and insurers; FISMA, which tells the federal government how personal information must be secured and protected; and a whole alphabet soup of politicians and industry leaders trying to force organizations into thinking about the big picture instead of keeping their noses down while focused on only one task.

It might be useful to present an example of the advantages that come with a focus on the big picture rather than the minutiae of security. Let's open up a scenario that actually happened and was illustrated by a 2005 InfoWorld article on identity management (http://www. infoworld.com/d/security-central/how-harry-met-sally-our-identity-management-test-bed-505). This was certainly an early effort to highlight the reality that identity management could no longer be a single system but must rather be a collection of systems—a collection that can potentially be geographically separated. The tested scenario also pointed out that, as IT systems affect more and more of the enterprise, the integration of these systems is a must, rather than a wish. The critical point herein is that one of the vendors involved in the test demonstrated the extent to which the integration of identity systems could potentially solve inherent weaknesses in both physical and information security.

> *The scenario is where a card swipe for physical access by itself isn't a security problem, and neither is a VPN authentication from a foreign country. However, in this case the card swipe and the VPN connection were for the same person. The particular identity management vendor's product combined the two events and the correlation was that the person couldn't have possibly been in two different places at the same time, and was thusly was a security breach.*
>
> (*Source:* http://www.infoworld.com/d/security-central/how-harry-met-sally-our-identity-management-test-bed-505)

What surprised us was how quickly these stand-alone identity management vendors were absorbed into larger organizations specifically for the integration of location- and correlation-aware identity management into network operating systems. It is now rare to have any major system that isn't physically capable of correlating physical location with systems security. Given that nearly a decade has passed since this landmark article was published, we now have network operating systems spread across multiple geographic locations and, in some cases, multiple continents. Even if someday we have systems spread across multiple planetary systems, the same basic principles apply. The security profile is tied to the identity but also needs to be correlated with physical location awareness.

Location Aware—Hardware or software that uses any of several techniques to determine its geographic location. The precision of the system can vary widely, depending on the requirements of the application.

Correlation Aware—Most often applied to database systems, this term means that the application or system is aware of the relationships that exist between different streams or sets of information. This implies that the correlation-aware system will have access to all the data it must be aware of. The level and degree of correlation can range from the very simple to the enormously complex, with processing power one of the limiting factors in many cases.

On our path to location-aware but not necessarily location-dependent security, it first became necessary to have a way to authenticate users unequivocally, but not in a way that required massive amounts of computing requirements overwhelming the client system. As a historical point of fact, this idea became possible for the information technology industry in 1961 at the University of Hawai'i at Manoa. Dr. Wesley Peterson published a paper on *Error Correcting Codes* (http://en.wikipedia.org/wiki/W._Wesley_Peterson) that laid out the theory on using mathematical algorithms for the purpose of error correction of data. The paper became the basis for all modern error correction systems and all modern encryption. This is significant because for the first time a person could test for *any* changes to a piece of data, whether it was observational oceanography acoustics or nuclear launch codes. It wasn't until much later that computing power would progress to the point that ubiquitous computing equipment such as mobile phones, laptops, or even entry control systems were being produced with enough computing power to take advantage of strong encryption for identity management.

Strong Encryption—In theory, encryption that is impossible to defeat in a reasonable amount of time using currently available techniques. In practice, this refers to encryption based on long (256 bit) keys, using algorithms that have proven themselves resistant to defeat using any currently available process.

Strong encryption has been, and will for the foreseeable future be, the key to uniquely identifying individuals regardless of whether the authentication system involves password keychains, files, or databases implemented at the individual, system, or organization level. Single key encryption (in which the same authentication string is used for both encryption and decryption) has been the bread and butter of most authentication systems up until the turn of the 21st century, but it would be a development at the Massachusetts Institute of Technology (MIT) by Ron Rivest, Adi Shamir, and Leonard Adelman (http://en.wikipedia.org/wiki/RSA_%28algorithm%29) that cracked the problem of having one key to encrypt and another to decrypt. The so-called *dual key encryption problem* (http://en.wikipedia.org/wiki/Cryptography) had been the holy grail of mathematicians for centuries, with efforts going back to locksmiths in the Victorian era. Simply put, two keys were required for every secure communications. A *private key* (known only to the sender) was used to encrypt the data, and a publicly available *public key* was used to decrypt it, with the result being a trustworthy way to validate the identity of the sender. Secure communications back to the "sender" would have the process reversed so that only the holder of the *private key* could un-encrypt the piece of data, regardless of whether others had copies of the *public key*.

We really can't remember or find a reference indicating who first started implementing location-aware security (though we have found references to location-aware security devices (http://www.theregister.co.uk/2006/10/27/altiris_client_sec/) as early as 2006 and to location-aware computing[1] as early as 2000), but it required a surge in computing power to process the data and the availability of near-ubiquitous network communications to provide the data and the opportunity to deliver it for processing. The entire notion of location-aware computing rose across a number of different computing areas roughly simultaneously; an example of a different application of the technology is Geotargeting (http://en.wikipedia.org/wiki/Geotargeting) for Internet marketing.[2] In each of these cases, and others in different arenas, the key technologies brought together presented a way to approximate physical locations (whether that involved cell-phone tower triangulation, GPS coordinates, or WiFi access point heat mapping) and the ability to correlate that physical location to a rule or set of rules for system behavior.

One of the first times we remember seeing geotargeting for security purposes was during a presentation by Symantec on their method for correlating Internet attacks with physical location for the purpose of "getting

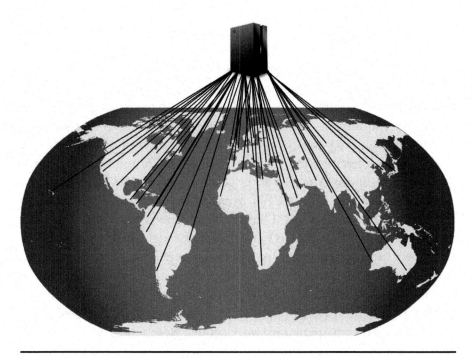

Figure 2.1. DDoS attacks can come from nearly every continent and nation simultaneously.

ahead of the attack" as it would sweep across the globe. The technology has certainly shown up in geotargeted marketing for pop-up ads, email spam, and many other forms of marketing to targeted consumers. The point here is that geolocation can be used for many different things, but, in our case, geotargeting also means that we have a fighting chance at figuring out where on the Internet a person is coming from for purposes such as global load balancing or to help localize sources of DDoS attacks, such as those shown in Figure 2.1.

Everything in the preceding few paragraphs is really is all about how to identify physical location in order to correlate security policies with concepts such as "trusted locations" (branch offices, secured home networks, etc.) that have had risk assessments performed and are considered relatively safe due to the levels of security in place. The risk assessment performed on trusted places should include the following:

- Deciding on a level of deep packet inspection and whether software for the firewall/IDS/IPS is updated frequently. You get what you pay for, and while the branch office may not need the same firewall/ IDS/IPS as the central office, it would certainly make sense to have a scaled-down unit that can still meet the safety standards of the larger organization.

- Is your VPN traffic appearing directly inside your trusted network or do you force it through a separate firewall zone so that you can have much finer control over what data is allowed to traverse your firewall? Implementing separate zones allows for more granular firewall rules in order to balance access with safety. Just because someone is coming across a VPN from behind another firewall doesn't mean their traffic is safe. One of our favorite sayings (yes, it's a long list) is "Trust but test" so that you're not caught with your knickers down because a malicious payload is delivered from a trusted source.

The location-specific nature of the security we're discussing can be as large as a country, as stationary as an office, or as tightly targeted as a specific device on a particular network subnet. Researchers within the US Department of Defense frequently have a demonstrable need for remote access to some relatively sensitive DoD networks for the purpose of transferring encrypted files. In this case, they've taken extraordinary measures to ensure that this traveler's computing platform (laptop) is secure and an acceptable risk. Many of these extraordinary measures are wrapped within a larger framework of layered security organized in such a way that a trusted computing platform is created. Let's take a moment to look at some of the layers and how they work together to create a more trustworthy computing environment.

Layered Security

A fairly recent development in the portable computing marketplace is the integration of a Trusted Platform Module (TPM) (http://en.wikipedia. org/wiki/Trusted_Platform_Module) that has the ability to work with emerging disk drives featuring built-in whole disk encryption. With features varying by manufacturer, the TPM typically has the ability to lock the entire platform if a password isn't provided, and in the case of emerging operating systems (Windows® 8), it has the ability to also store additional pieces of security data to be used for multifactor authentication. This very targeted, very recent layered technology (in which password access to the entire system is laid atop encrypted, lockable data storage within the system) is an extension of much earlier layered security approaches developed for minicomputers.

Security layers were implemented in the 1970s by Wang Scientific Corporation with their Wang VS operating system. To the best of our knowledge, this was the first operating system that allowed for credential proxies whereby security rules could be applied to applications, rather than to users. There have always been situations in which an application might need to look up a potentially sensitive piece of information that was beyond the authorized access of the current user but was necessary to the task. In the case of the Wang VS, the application did the lookup in order to properly validate the issue under question but never let the user touch or view the sensitive information. The proxy concept has since become widespread for systems and application software as a means of allowing access to the logical results of comparisons and data lookups without giving more access authority than is necessary to an individual or group of users.

Within this two-paragraph history lesson are lessons about the progression of encryption and the overall reliability and safety of systems now available for remote users. Cloud computing comes down to *everything* being available from remote locations. As a result, care needs to be exercised when balancing risk with usability. Designing in management and troubleshooting visibility is key to success with an emphasis on testing to make sure your basic assumptions about the nature of risk and requirements for access were correct. What we're really talking about is a variable number of best practices that you have to make educated decisions on. Defense in depth and "trust but test" are all about layers and control points in your system, regardless of whether you gain access through a walk down the hall or a link to the public cloud. Cloud security might be a shiny new model, but it is based upon tried and true methodologies with reasonable and logical extensions that deal with the cloud's unique issues.

Looking Forward

Balancing risk versus access has been the challenge of every IT professional globally, and clouds should be viewed as the final exam. You don't control 100% of the infrastructure of most cloud computing infrastructures, and you don't control the pipes used to reach them. So what you really need to do is make sure your house is in order so that when you connect to the "foreign" system you can trust your overall environment. *Never* blindly trust, always test, since you never know when a misunderstanding by someone on your team might accidentally leave a security hole. Here's a favored methodology that has been used on installations all over the world:

- Build your system plan by first making sure that your entire team knows the end game. Think of this as an organizational mission statement to ensure that your whole team has a better chance at working towards a common goal instead of getting lost in pet projects.
- Lay out a timeline document that describes which pieces of the project depend upon others, and which pieces need to be in place before others can be built.
- Make sure your team describes how they're going to achieve their portion of the project in the team's native language. We're a strong believer in the saying that you can't possibly automate a task that you don't know how to do manually. This is where I love to send my team members into the various departments to sit with the users and actually learn how to do the process. If they can't describe the process in a human language, they can't possibly succeed with technology.
- As a team, poke holes in one another's descriptions and document how the team thinks each section can be tested and, most importantly, how that portion might be broken. This is where you need to encourage people to think of how to break the system so that, as a team, you can defend your system against people that don't have anything better to do than try to break in.
- Lay out an acceptance plan for each module and actually try to break it. Test, test, and test again means less egg on your face than if a customer finds the problem.
- Do you have change management (http://en.wikipedia.org/wiki/Change_management) set up? That white board is fine if everyone is together in a bullpen, but what if you're hiring programmers in another country for some modules? Taking the time to make sure you use something like Git (http://en.wikipedia.org/wiki/Git_(software)) and making sure you configure the dependencies

between modules can go a long way towards reducing breakage due to updates.

- Make every attempt to find out what kind of workload your management is thinking about, and triple it. Most systems work just fine with your team banging away at it, but what happens when you hit the system with synthetic load from something like "webload" (http://www.radview.com/product/description-overview.aspx/)?

- Testing also gives you a good idea of the point where you must think about load sharing. Does your application allow for multiple instances to share a common backend? Can you bring up multiple copies of the "widget works" ecommerce site, and what does this do to your system? Do you need to think about some sort of dedicated network to link these systems together just to make sure record locking never gets blocked by too much incoming traffic?

- Do you need to ask your cloud provider for another virtual switch (vSwitch) just for your apps to talk to some sort of controller app?

- Did you forget backups? Not every cloud provider is going to give you full access to your data store. Do you have to ship a big USB drive to your provider to get those snapshots backed up?

- Are you planning on using a VPN? If so, do you have public IP address space or Network Address Translation (NAT) in your cloud system? Using a non-routable private address space (http://en.wikipedia.org/wiki/Private_network) and coordinating it across your sites means that your VPN policies don't break if you have duplicate networks on both sides.

- Did you allow for storage of master data copies in your storage requests? Did you allow for enough resources to bring up "draft" machines? This way, once you go into production you have a way to test changes before you commit.

- Finally, don't let the deadline be an excuse for poor documentation. In a cloud you don't always have the same visibility as you might in your own data center. We can't tell you how many times we've run into programmers who use insanely cryptic module names, variables, etc. Make your team read one another's documentation, and make sure they know that speaking up isn't personal. God forbid that someone gets hit by a truck, but that's the attitude you MUST take. No one should be indispensable: If some members on the team can't understand other members' documentation, it means that if something breaks, the time to fix it will increase exponentially.

References

1. Priyantha, N. B., Chakraborty, A., and Balakrishnan, H. (2000). "The Cricket Location-Support System." *Proceedings of the 6th Annual International Conference on Mobile Computing and Networking*, August 6–11, 2000, Boston, MA, 32–43.
2. Svantesson, D. J. B. (2004). "Geo-Location Technologies and Other Means of Placing Borders on the 'Borderless' Internet." Retrieved from http://epublications.bond.edu.au/law_pubs/63

Chapter 3

The Basics of IT Security: From Mainframe to Cloud

In this chapter, we begin to examine the nature of security and what it means for IT, regardless of whether that IT is in the classic mainframe and client model or the latest iteration of cloud computing. We can take this broad approach because, as we'll see, the basics of IT security are rather consistent from one type of computing to another. We'll follow this with a look at two of the foundation pieces of any type of security: a definition of precisely what it is that we want to secure, followed by a definition of what we mean when we use the word "security." It's very tempting, in both these cases, to fall back on tautologies or overly simplistic lists. Either is a mistake.

One of the overarching themes of this book is that careful thought put into concept development and planning stages pays off when it comes to implementation. That is no where more true than at the beginning. So, as "Do-re-mi" instructs, let's start at the very beginning. . . .

The Unchanging Nature of IT Security

The essential nature of securing IT infrastructure and data hasn't changed since the early days of mainframe computers. What do we mean by this? There are two key points that have remained the same since data processing began:

- Ensure that only those properly authorized have access to the system and the data it contains.
- Ensure that those properly authorized are only able to conduct those transactions for which they have authorization.

That's it, really. If you can guarantee that those two conditions are being met, you can close the book, declare your work done, and call it a day. The trouble, of course, is that each of those two simple-sounding items contains a multitude of troublesome details that must be worked out against a backdrop of legions that would try to defeat your best efforts.

The only real changes have been in the technology to be protected, the scope of what must be protected, and the technology available with which the valuable assets can be protected. Oh, yes, and there has been some evolution in the threats against which the systems much be protected. In these respects, there are elements of this book that will be applicable to any IT architecture, regardless of whether it involves cloud computing. In other respects, though, cloud computing presents new options and challenges for the IT professional precisely because of the technology and scope involved.

Technology changes within IT are important for security because they have done so much to make it more difficult, if not downright impossible, for physical access control to solve the majority of computer security problems. Think of it: In the days of IT yore, computers were something that users went to visit. Today, computing is, almost literally, wherever you happen to be. Authorized access has evolved from something that was primarily a function of physical locks and uniformed security guards to a process designed to make sure that a given user is, in fact, who he or she claims to be. Multifactor authentication, in which the individuals trying to access the system must provide something they have (typically their name), something they know (typically a password), and even something they "are" (generally speaking, a fingerprint, retina pattern, or face that is recognized by the system) is now the norm when it comes to gaining access to a computer system or its data. Of course, things are complicated somewhat when the "user" trying to gain access is a machine or computer system rather than a human.

At first blush, it might seem that guaranteeing the identity of a computer would be much simpler than vouching for the true identity of a duplicitous human being. In practice, though, computer-to-computer authentication presents its own set of challenges and a set of risks that are considerable when taken together. Part of the problem, of course, is that we've been so conditioned to think of machines and systems as inherently trustworthy. The aura of trust is part of what makes "man in the middle" attacks, in which an unauthorized system intercepts communications and either allows unknown individuals to steal information or redirects and changes information, substituting incorrect data for the proper information sent (and expected) by authorized users, so dangerous. This type of attack, in which internal components (or malicious systems masquerading as internal components) are the antagonistic vectors, points out another aspect of modern security that creates difficulty for those protecting systems and data: IT security is now a 360-degree activity.

One of the important factors to understand early on is that security is a "360-degree" issue. Far too many individuals focus only on protecting IT assets from criminals and malicious organizations that lie outside the company. It is just as important to protect assets from intentional and accidental loss due to the action (or inaction) of individuals inside the company. Let's now look at some of the essential elements of security, whether clouds are part of the IT infrastructure or not . . .

The first element of security is the knowledge of precisely what it is you're securing. Of course, you want everything within your control to be safe and secure, but security in the real world recognizes that the penalties for the loss of some assets are far greater than the penalties for the loss of others.

Next comes defining what security means for the elements you're securing. Although it might seem to be simple, we'll see that "security" is a term that can mean different things in different situations. Knowing what you're trying to accomplish can have a remarkable effect on your ability to succeed.

Once you've settled on what you're securing and what security means, then you can begin the work of accomplishing a secure environment.

Much of this book is going to look at different ways of making an environment secure, but before we start down that path, there's one more critical piece of information you need to have. Put simply, it is that the label "private" doesn't mean anything involved is actually "secure."

One of the great debates in cloud computing concerns the difference between public cloud architectures, private clouds, and hybrid clouds that have both public and private cloud services within the total system. Some people (often, to be sure, people associated with private cloud vendors) will argue that private cloud components are inherently more secure than public cloud infrastructure. In this book, we argue that the details of security implementation vary between the two types of cloud services, but that one is not automatically more or less secure than the other. The basic issues of security are the same no matter how the cloud service is provided.

The reason we bring this up is that there's a temptation to relax a bit when implementing an application on a platform that is described as "private." This temptation is related to the drive to overindulge in a food labeled "low calorie." What seems sensible may leave you open to unfortunate consequences if you forget that the basic rules of security apply whether you're talking about physical premises access, a public cloud infrastructure, or a private cloud.

Define What You Need to Secure

It's easy to say, "We need to secure everything!" But that's not a particularly useful answer. Instead, you should know precisely what it is that you're trying to secure, exactly why, and what the consequences of failing to secure the thing would be. This can be more complicated than common sense might imply.

Take data, for instance. You obviously will want to secure all your customer data. Do you know precisely what information from and about your customers you store? Do you know precisely where every bit of that data is stored? Are you sure? With the advent of the mobile workforce, it's quite common for IT professionals to have only the broadest notion of what customer data they're storing, and only the most cursory concept of where every copy of the data resides at any given moment.

For many professionals, that issue of "every copy" is one that became important as a topic in database management and gained importance as mobile devices grew like mushrooms after a spring rain in the enterprise

IT ecosystem. What once was a key concept in data rationalization has become one of the most important considerations in IT security. It's so important, we should take a paragraph or two and devote special attention to it.

There are some who consider data copied onto mobile devices the single biggest issue in data security today. A bill introduced in the US Senate—the Personal Data Protection and Breach Accountability Act of 2011—proposed harsh penalties for those who copied data onto mobile devices that were then lost, and required companies with substantial quantities of sensitive customer data to prove compliance with security and privacy protection policies. Others, however, feel that the issue isn't with the security of data copied onto mobile devices, it's with the fact that the copying is taking place at all.

Writing in SANS NewsBites, editor Marcus Ranum said, "the underlying cause of data leakage is not that it's 'securely stored' it's that it's duplicated into too many people's hands— people who proceed to copy it to a thumb drive or laptop which is then lost. The problem is not securing a copy of the data; it's securing data against copying."[1] Cloud computing may actually provide enhanced security in this regard, because it allows *access* to data without requiring *local copies* of that data.

Of course, securing data on the cloud is its own problem, but you know that—it's why you're reading this book, after all. The truth is, though, that security of a single copy of data on a single repository is an order of magnitude simpler a problem than securing a near-limitless number of data copies on devices that you might or might not control with any degree of certainty. The first step, then, in securing the cloud is making sure that the cloud is where the data to be secured is located. Once you've done that, your job is much easier. But what if the politics of your organization won't allow that: What then?

Take a moment to think about this and relate it to the physical assets your organization holds. Many, if not most, pieces of physical property are protected by locks and keys that work based on keeping assets on one side of a door and unauthorized users on the other side. Certain other assets are protected through locks and keys, even though they might well operate beyond the walls of the organization. Different rates of loss were assumed for the two types of assets because of the difficulty of knowing the precise location of highly mobile assets, but technology has now enabled the ability for companies to track their assets regardless of location through GPS tagging and similar strategies.

Some enterprise IT professionals remain locked in a mindset analogous to the physical asset "locked behind a wall" era. Whereas there are some pieces of data that must continue to receive that level of protection, most modern organizations have data that, although sensitive, must be "in the field" to be of maximum value. For that data, a set of techniques similar to the key of an automobile is required, along with technologies analogous to the GPS asset tracker. For both these tools, a cloud-based solution will be where many organizations turn to build a protection strategy. Of course, you still need to have a solid idea of where your data is if you're going to offer adequate protection.

As if knowing where all the data is stored weren't challenging enough, can you accurately point to every piece of IT infrastructure? Are you sure? If you allow employees to work from home, or to access information from cell phones, their own personal computers, or computers at customer sites or hotel business centers, do you consider those computers (and their associated routers, switches, and storage units) part of your IT infrastructure? Why not? The fact is that every piece of equipment that can create a connection to one or more of your servers, and every piece of data that can be shared with those pieces of equipment, becomes part of your corporate IT infrastructure. If you aren't working to protect each one of them, you haven't broadened your definition of "IT" sufficiently.

Define What Security Means

In a later chapter of this book we'll explore the possibilities that exist for extending data protection from the cloud onto the various devices that might live somewhere outside the enterprise firewall. One of the things that we'll rapidly be faced with is the question of how we'll define security on the mobile devices. Are you required to somehow prevent the loss of the devices that contain the data? Are the handcuffs and chains usually associated with nuclear launch codes to become required security equipment for enterprise tablets and smart phones? If not, where do you draw the line?

Many organizations will find that they don't really get to decide where the line is drawn: Regulators are ready, bold marker in hand, to draw it for them. The first job in looking at a definition of security, then, is figuring out whether the definition has been established with no input from you or anyone in your organization.

Depending on the nature of the business, you might well find that you are subject to multiple regulatory privacy and security definitions. Regulatory requirements are frequently (though not always) complementary, and they always carry with them the requirement that an organization prove that it is in compliance with those regulations. In the process of examining regulatory requirements, you're likely to find yourself faced with an elaborate Venn diagram of regulatory obligations. The most interesting cases—the ones that will require attention far in excess of the sheer number of records involved—will be those that lie in the intersection of multiple regulations. Some of these, to be fair, will not be amenable to cloud security at all, or will only be amenable to treatment by certain varieties of cloud (a private cloud owned and within the protection of the organization, for example). Even if only part of the organization has its security strategy dictated for it, virtually every group will have to determine where it draws the security line and the shape the area within the line will take.

The medium for drawing that line (wherever you decide it belongs) is increasingly found in Mobile Device Management (MDM) software. MDM software began as a collection of blunt-force instruments allowing enterprise IT departments to encrypt entire devices, require password policy enforcement, or erase the contents of devices in the event of theft or hacking attempts. Later-generation MDM has become more sophisticated, allowing for individual files or applications to be locked by passwords and encrypted, located, and even erased through a cloud-based set of technologies and strategies. How does the cloud do this? There are a couple of key strategies in use.

The first is to use MDM as a way of enforcing a requirement that data be stored in a cloud-based system rather than on the local device. This has a significant impact on the ability to protect data because it helps deal with the "do you know where your data is stored" question we asked some paragraphs ago. That sort of policy enforcement, regardless of where the device in question is located, is a key advantage of cloud-based security for mobile devices. The second key strategy doesn't involve policy enforcement as much as adding a capability that is far more cumbersome without a cloud.

Traditional computers and computing devices have been protected from many threats through software loaded onto the computer itself. The anti-malware software that has become a standard part of client system operating environments is less desirable in the somewhat more limited confines of a mobile device. Assigning the protection functions to the cloud and ensuring that all mobile operations are conducted under the protective cover of that cloud, makes for more productive devices and more responsive device protection, since a modification to protection can be enacted once and immediately pushed to cover all the mobile devices in the organization's fleet.

Next up is creating a definition of what security means for your infrastructure and data. Preventing "bad things" from happening may or may not be sufficient for your situation, but in a growing number of situations it's only the beginning. We have already discussed the factors that may bear on data security, but infrastructure—the "streets and buildings" in which the data moves and lives—has become no less complex than the data itself.

Much of the analysis already discussed around data will also apply to infrastructure. In particular, the issues around regulatory and legal compliance extend from data to the infrastructure on which it is stored. There is a critical difference though, and it is a difference that will extend into the world of the cloud.

An organization's data is typically defined by and controlled by the organization itself. It is exceptionally rare, however, for an organization to build its own infrastructure components. There is a great extent, therefore, to which infrastructure security must be ensured through a partnership between an organization and the vendors supplying its infrastructure components. As we will see in later chapters, security for infrastructure components and systems may depend as much upon an organization's ability to communicate requirements (and codify those requirements in legal agreements) as upon its technical capabilities. The good news is that the experience gained in working with infrastructure vendors can be exploited when reaching agreements for cloud security. The bad news is that deficiencies in the definition and communication abilities will be amplified when moving from traditional infrastructure to the cloud.

One critical piece of the overall security puzzle is that cloud applications and infrastructure should be thoroughly tested, just as traditional applications and infrastructure should be tested, on a regular basis. It's especially important that a type of testing called penetration testing (tests in which a team of experts tries to penetrate the system security) be performed before you take the leap into a significant cloud application infrastructure. One of the most common complaints concerning enterprise security is that corporations don't test anymore. At one time, large editorial tests done at InfoWorld and other computer industry publications drew a host of fans screaming for copies of the test plans so that they could recreate the work internally. This just isn't the case anymore, and the authors feel strongly that the pendulum needs to find a bit of middle ground here. Testing tools and implementations can be quite expensive, but one should at least run some attacks against any production system in a friendly environment before it is exposed to the rather hostile world in which it will live.

If you gather from this that there can be a significant payoff to learning the lessons of infrastructure security, then you've already made an important first step. Now we can begin to explore the specifics of securing the cloud.

Security Review

Let's review what we've learned in this chapter before we begin applying these basics to the specifics of security of, by, and for the cloud.

The most basic security concepts haven't changed dramatically since the earliest days of computing.

- Ensure that only those properly authorized have access to the system and the data it contains.
- Ensure that those properly authorized are only able to conduct those transactions for which they have authorization.

Everything that happens in the realm of security, from the simplest file-use policy to the most complex encryption algorithm, will be put to use in the service of these two key needs. Precisely how all of the various tools are used will depend on how an organization goes through two processes that are broad in concept but deep in specific execution.

Define What Needs to Be Secured

An enterprise of any size will generate a vast amount of data, ranging from the critical and highly sensitive to the trivial. Do the plans for an upcoming departmental picnic require the same level of protection that customer credit card numbers are given? In most cases the answer is "no." Deciding which data is protected to which level is critical and begins with the step of determining precisely what data the organization possesses and where that data currently resides. Once those facts are obtained, the next stage of security planning can begin.

Determine What "Security" Means

Once you know what all your data is and where it resides, you can begin to decide what to do to protect each type or piece of data. That means looking at protecting the data itself, protecting the servers and clients on which it may be stored and processed, and protecting the networks and other means via which data is transferred. Regulations and legal definitions may impose requirements other than those that your organization develops internally, and the combination of internal and external compliance (and proving each of those) must be taken into account in any security plan.

After a plan is decided upon and implemented, it should be thoroughly tested so that any deficiencies or weaknesses can be discovered and mitigated before they can be exploited by those outside the organization. These steps of decision, implementation, and testing will determine just how secure any cloud-based architecture will be.

References

1. Ranum, M., SANS Newsbites, Vol. 13, Issue 23. Retrieved from https://www.sans.org/newsletters/newsbites/newsbites.php?vol=13&issue=73&rss=Y

Chapter 4

The Basics of Security Failure

Let's get this straight: Computers and their related equipment are pretty dumb. They only do what you tell them to do. Even quite a few "act of God" events can be traced back to pushing systems beyond their design capabilities. Many remaining acts of God can be credited to the simple fact that fallible humans wrote the software. Remember that some of the first Atlas rockets had to be destroyed right after liftoff because a programmer forgot a semicolon at the end of a line, and it's obvious that a little error can have huge consequences.

When security fails, it's normally because someone either had a lack of imagination or simply forgot something. This is why the military around the world preaches "defense in depth," so that mistakes don't get people killed. Layer, layer, and layer again is good security practice, whether you're protecting a database or a military installation. We know a whole lot of folks who run Secure Sockets Layers (SSLs) over virtual private networks (VPNs) and also have to go through a firewall zone to get to the servers. Defense in depth means that if someone leaks the VPN key, he or she still has to figure out how to do a man-in-the-middle attack (http://en.wikipedia.org/wiki/Man-in-the-middle_attack) to get into the SSL stream. Then, hopefully, the intrusion prevention system (IPS) will catch them as the traffic crosses from the VPN zone to the trusted server zone, which has a directory-based server login, such as Active Directory, as well as group access policies to directories as the last line of defense. Each line of defense needs to reinforce the other, and each has to be a best effort.

Defense in depth is important because, although firewalls have become fairly effective, hackers are changing their tactics in response. Hackers commonly use social engineering to construct amazingly good malicious emails that tantalize users into clicking on a link to malware that infects their network from the inside. In a 2009 InfoWorld article on firewalls (http://www.infoworld.com/d/security-central/malware-fighting-firewalls-miss-mark-751), we purposely ran the attacks backwards in anticipation of just this situation. We literally ran the kitchen sink and hit the subject firewalls with the entire list of CERT attacks (http://en.wikipedia.org/wiki/Computer_emergency_response_team) from both the inside and outside, then measured how much legitimate traffic could still get through. It amazed us to see that nearly all the products were well protected against attacks from the outside, but folded up when attacked from the inside.

To protect against these "advanced persistent threats," many practitioners now suggest that organizations separate major internal functions into zones, so that appropriate firewall rules can be applied to not only protect against external malware, but also to help protect against the actions of trusted employees who clicked on a bad guy–sponsored link.

Policy First

Although we're preaching to the choir, let's talk just a bit about the ramifications of not taking the time to set up at least the barest framework of a security policy. Just the process of developing a policy forces the manager or organization to think through the moving parts of your security system and the ways in which the parts overlap and depend upon each other. Just like a good database design, mapping the relations and interdependencies can go a long way toward mitigating the accidental breaking of associated pieces through an understanding of how those pieces work together.

Our favorite example of the dangers of not thinking the policy through comes from a major university's IT group, which had a nasty habit of ignoring the mainframe support staff as they migrated away from big iron. So, when a change to the Lightweight Directory Access Protocol (LDAP) authentication system was made, warnings about mainframe systems being affected were unheeded. Although the student registration system was based upon network resources, the main student information system was still on the mainframe in Customer Information Control System (CICS). The simple schema change in LDAP resulted in a week's worth of registration data becoming invalidated. Recovery was time consuming, and the lesson learned nearly cost the IT manager's job.

Let's look at some of the moving parts and how small changes can affect the whole. First and foremost, authentication systems and Single Sign On (SSO) are by far the biggest moving parts in any front-line application security system. Each seat at the table represents a client access license (CAL) in the Microsoft world. This translates into a sufficiently large investment to make huge organizations, such as universities, hesitant to implement a Microsoft directory authentication system (e.g., Active Directory®). Why? Even the seemingly tiny investment of $15 per student (this is an estimated academic volume license: the real pricing is considered confidential by terms of the academic End User License Agreement [EULA]) seems small until you multiply it by a student population in excess of 50K at many universities. That numbers swells to nearly 500K, if you add in alumni, as most universities are doing today. Now, let's look at what this means if you're in a similar-sized organization considering a move to a public cloud infrastructure.

Moving to a public cloud means you need to think about how your users will authenticate; do you have enough network bandwidth and is your latency low enough that the user experience won't suffer? Microsoft's answer is to carve off a read-only portion of the Active Directory schema on a per site basis. But what is the security exposure when a large portion of your user credentials are no longer under your direct control (http://technet.microsoft.com/en-us/library/cc749943.aspx on AD design issues)?

One huge issue that almost everyone forgets is that although authentication is now encrypted (hopefully, though there are still too many exceptions), software such as Remote Desktop™ or even Citrix® desktop sessions aren't always implemented with end-to-end encryption. More to the point is that older (but more widely compatible) versions of Remote Desktop send out login information in clear text. Is the unencrypted data flying back and forth sensitive? The real question may be even more basic.

When was the last time you thought carefully about the data moving back and forth between web portals and servers? Is your entire web portal for Human Resources (HR) (leave applications, customer relationship management [CRM], etc.) fully or partially encrypted? Users continue to have a bad habit of clicking "yes" in response to far too many dialog boxes, especially if they think the question is coming from a trusted site. A particularly worrisome issue is that "man-in-the-middle" (MITM) attacks have become all too easy to implement with scripts based on Squid/Ettercap/etc., which are available to hackers in the wild. The first part of a MITM attack involves inserting the MITM machine into the conversation.

Many criminal systems use the concept of ARP poisoning, so that the workstation now talks to one network interface and the destination/router talks to another, in much the same way that a legitimate web proxy functions. The MITM system will then use its position in the transaction chain to poison the ARP tables (http://en.wikipedia.org/wiki/ARP_spoofing) of the computers on each end of the transaction and push the Ethernet address of the new (criminal controlled) network interface in their place (see Figure 4.1). Because no normal computer user is going to even know how to pay attention to the Ethernet address of his or her router, the hacker can now use the MITM software to watch the conversation go by.

A particularly scary example of an MITM attack (http://en.wikipedia.org/wiki/Man_in_the_middle_attack) was demonstrated when a Secure ID-authenticated electronic trading transaction was changed from a purchase of one stock into the purchase of another. Although this is a very specific example to demonstrate a new multifactor authentication system, the attack did exist and it did work.

Getting to the point, no rational human is going to keep track of IP address changes that are the hallmark of a MITM attack, but this kind of detail is exactly what computers are good for. Intrusion Detection systems (IDS) have long had MITM detection capability (most firewalls flag it as ARP spoofing), so it's just a matter of making sure that your IDS can view enough of your network traffic to actually see the MITM in action. In clouds, just as in your internal network, detection relies upon being able to see the traffic, which means that the security team needs to have the time and resources to deploy sensors into the network (or cloud) at key locations.

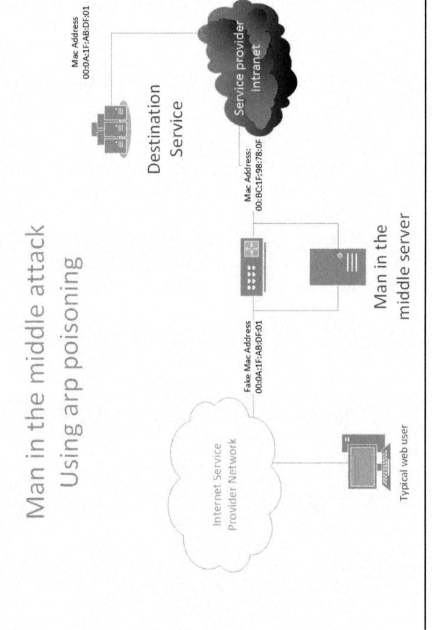

Figure 4.1. A theoretical "Man-in-the-Middle" attack.

Real and Virtual Taps

In the cloud, you now have vSwitches (http://en.wikipedia.org/wiki/ VMware_ESX; Wikipedia is inaccurate in this case because vSwitches are a feature of all the major server virtualization systems on the market today) and top of rack networks to contend with—equipment that customers may or may not have diagnostic access to. Here, vendors such as NetScout, Network Instruments, and Gigamon have all risen to the occasion with software versions of their taps and probes for taking a direct look at the traffic on virtual switches.

When we start discussing the ability to look at key segments of the network, the knee jerk reaction in the world of network monitoring is to save a few dollars by only using SPANs/mirror (http://en.wikipedia. org/wiki/Port_mirroring) ports on existing switches; but you have to be extremely careful in just how many ports you plan on mirroring to avoid oversubscription. Determining whether a series of taps or ports is oversubscribed is a relatively simple process: Add up the bandwidth of all the ports you're going to mirror and see if the total is equal to or less than the bandwidth of the tap or aggregating port. For example, five 100 Mb/s ports (full duplex is looking at both sides of the conversation) to a single gigabit port is fine, but two or more gigabit mirror ports could potentially oversubscribe your gigabit mirror/span port.

A similar problem can be found when aggregating taps where the traffic from both sides of the network transaction is aggregated onto a single test instrument connection. This particular situation was a loophole that an attorney was exploiting to get data captures for cases that used aggregating taps thrown out of court. A paper published at the 2007 IFIP (International Federation of Information Processing Societies working group 11.9) by Brian Chee, Barbary Endicott-Popvsky, and Deborah Frincke (http://academic.research.microsoft.com/Publication/4284232/ calibration-testing-of-network-tap-devices) provided guidelines for predicting conditions that would create oversubscription conditions and potentially corrupt data streams being gathered for court cases.

It's easy to see how a comprehensive monitoring scheme for a high-speed network could easily oversubscribe the available span ports on the core router. One strategy for dealing with this problem has been demonstrated over the last three decades by the Interop™ tradeshow Network Operations Center (NOC) team in the form of a physically isolated network just for network analysis. This simple secondary network (traditionally created as a flat non-routed network) was set aside specifically for devices such as console servers, SNMP monitoring systems, and taps. This "spy" network provides out-of-band management (OOBI: out-of-band infrastructure) (http://en.wikipedia.org/wiki/OOBI) for the InteropNET and has time and again proven its value. For instance, when the Slammer denial of service attack hit the InteropNET, the team was able to use the spy network to characterize the attack and apply access control language at the upstream routers to prevent the attack from further affecting the tradeshow network.

The whole concept of out-of-band management networks gained acceptance as devices such as serial console servers and IP KVMs became necessary when data centers exploded in size and complexity. By physically separating this "Hail Mary" network from the production infrastructure, engineers prevent in-band attacks from locking them out of the enterprise

Figure 4.2. Opengear cellular routers. (*Source*: http://opengear.com/product-acm5000-g.html)

network. At the same time, by recycling old switches after an upgrade for use in the OOBI network, administrators get to keep the cost of this system within reason. Some companies, such as OpenGear (see Figure 4.2), have gone as far as creating management gateways that contain serial port servers, ethernet switches, and environmental sensors that have fall-back connections to the 3G and 4G world. So although you could certainly build something like this from an old machine and a new Linux® installation, what you most likely can't afford is the hardened Linux, turn key operation and ultra low power consumption that a purpose-built appliance can provide.

Understand the Causes of Security Failures

We're only human, and nowhere is this more evident than in security, where constant pounding by the bad guys tends to expose even the tiniest mistakes. When Windows Server® 2000 was the latest flower growing in Redmond, the InfoWorld Review Center crew found out that the average uncompromised life span of an unpatched Win2k server on the University of Hawaii network was around 45 seconds. In this case, the huge number of infected machines with bots on them took advantage of the unpatched machine to own it and turn it into yet another member of the malicious zombie army.

Face it, there are a lot of people out there with far too much time on their hands: They read the same books and attend the same conferences as legitimate IT professionals. The difference is that they have flexible morality and the time to write automated systems that can constantly search out machines with vulnerabilities and then infect them. The fact that this is a book on cloud computing and security is a good indication that clouds are not immune. The fact is that clouds are stationary targets, and it isn't very hard at all to discover the address space a cloud vendor is using and repeatedly probe that range until a vulnerability is found. The logic is similar to the reason why universities always seem to be infected; they tend to have huge data pipes and are big, fat stationary targets.

It could also be argued that a large number of breeches are caused by security exceptions that are created to accommodate a special project and then inadvertently left in place after the project is completed. It's not even that the IT department chooses to leave an exception in the security scheme; more likely, the IT group is never notified that the project has been completed and thus never knows to remove the special exception. (Yes, Victoria, change management is a good thing.)

We've also seen a significant gap between the human resources department and the IT group on the discipline of removing access credentials when an employee leaves the company or leaves the position that required a specific level of access. Credentials lying fallow means the passwords associated with the credentials aren't being changed and therefore provide hackers a stationary target for brute-force password cracking systems. The advent of graphics processing unit (GPU) desktop supercomputing means that massive amounts of cheap computing power have made brute force password cracking something anyone can afford (http://arstechnica. com/security/2012/12/25-gpu-cluster-cracks-every-standard-windows-password-in-6-hours/).

GPU-based cracking software is now commonplace on the Internet, and password cracks once thought to be beyond the reach of any but government crackers now take days instead of years to achieve. IT and HR must have a very close work relationship so that the attack of a disgruntled (former) employee who wants to delete project data can be mitigated simply by disabling his or her account. This way, the data can be preserved for future legitimate access, and only systems administrators can maintain access to intellectual property in the interim.

Understand the Consequences of Ineffective Security

On one level, it seems that the consequences of ineffective or inadequate security are quite simple to calculate: Without effective security, people steal your stuff. In the land of real consequences, though, simple theft may not be the worst outcome from security that doesn't get the job done. Data that isn't removed but rather copied for use in identity theft can cause huge damage to customers, employees, partners, and the company victimized by the breach. Repairing the damage can also be exceptionally expensive, with some analysts (Ponemon Institute) estimating that each affected record results in $202 of associated costs to the company. For breaches that can involve tens of thousands to millions of records, this can easily represent a massive expense to the company (http://www.ponemon. org/news-2/23).

With a growing number of companies falling under multiple regulatory regimes, the cost of failing to comply with those regulations can be enormous, regardless of whether an actual data breach results. HIPAA, GLBA, SarBox, PCI, and other regulations can impose massive financial penalties and mandated changes to the procedures and infrastructures involved. If a security breach does occur and involve what is determined to be a lack of compliance with regulations, then the $202 per record estimated earlier can quickly skyrocket into ruinous financial penalties.

In addition to the direct financial costs, indirect costs in the form of damaged reputations, lost business opportunities, and lost customer contacts can add substantial, if difficult to quantify, insult to the injury of the breach.

The following is an example from the manufacturer's point of view, in which Citrix has been struggling with these rapid changes and how these changes need to also affect security policies and their implementation:

> *Read any survey on cloud trends and you'll find security is inevitably listed as a top inhibitor to adoption. But what is really behind this concern and what can organizations do about it?*
>
> *For starters, recognize that cloud is a radical change for enterprise IT, and asks that years of hard-wired security thinking be undone. IT no longer owns everything, so it's natural that questions arise about control, policies, privacy and shared resources. That's not to say security concerns are unwarranted or to diminish the fact that a single cloud security breach can impact hundreds or even thousands of organizations. Yet, in reality, many public clouds are even more secure and evolved than the infrastructure that some companies currently have in place today.*
>
> *Another reason for the concern about cloud security is that changes are happening without IT's permission. Users are embracing the cloud unilaterally by bringing their own devices and solutions to work. Think SalesForce.com, data sharing apps or dev/test workloads running in Amazon EC2. Instead of resisting, IT should work with these bottoms-up cloud pioneers to understand what's driving them and see where internal services are falling short.*
>
> *Citrix believes that IT can embrace the cloud era with secure solutions for what people want—mobile workstyles and cloud services. Solutions such as Citrix CloudGateway and Citrix XenDesktop let IT maintain control while promoting the trends of consumerization and BYO. Similarly, Citrix CloudPlatform powered by Apache CloudStack provides on-demand infrastructure that isolates net-*

work, storage and compute resources from those of other tenants. As such, IT maintains control and gains efficiency, while users become more productive and mobile.

Looking forward, IT will see more workloads moving to the cloud and security will become implicit as industry standards evolve. Companies that embrace these changes now will evolve faster towards a mutually beneficial cloud strategy for the entire organization.

– Kurt Roemer, Chief Security Strategist at Citrix

Security failure isn't black and white but rather many shades of gray representing a multitude of mistakes. Thorough documentation, rigorous peer review, and change management, combined with open communications paths can go a long way towards making your cloud more secure. Remember, the military has long planned for human fallibility through extensive use of defense in depth; there is no reason why you can't learn from their experience.

Chapter 5

The Basics of Fitting Security to Situation

Security may have many qualities, but "one size fits all" is most certainly not among them. The basic principles of security must, therefore, be custom fitted to each situation so as to prevent two equally uncomfortable situations. The first result of badly fitting security is security that leaves gaps through which an attacker may enter. Just as a raincoat that fits poorly can leave streams of cold water coursing down the wearer's back, a security scheme that doesn't fit the situation can lead to cascading security failures through gaps in coverage. The second result of security that doesn't fit the situation can be even more dangerous than it is uncomfortable: A bad fit can lead to security that is far less effective than it appears, or is designed, to be. It is, to mangle a phrase, what you don't know that you don't know that can end up making itself known in the most dramatic and destructive way possible.

Understand the Price of Security

Understanding the cost of ineffective security is one piece of the analytical puzzle that is required to understand the business and strategy of security. The other major piece is figuring out exactly how much it will cost to

49

provide effective security. As with understanding the cost of security problems, this is not as straightforward a process as it might first appear.

Certainly the acquisition cost of security technology has to be taken into account, but as with so much of IT, the basic acquisition cost is rarely the most substantial piece of the overall price of the technology. There are considerable costs that can accrue in designing, implementing, and managing security. The monitoring and management aspects, in particular, require nontrivial expertise for meaningful action (or reaction) based on the data generated by the security system. This expertise is not static, and an organization with a computer security staff must be willing to commit resources to the ongoing education and training of those staff members.

In recent years, the price of security for many organizations has come to include the cost of proving, to the satisfaction of an auditing organization, that the security policies, procedures, and infrastructure of the organization are compliant with all relevant regulations under which the organization must operate. These regulatory pressures have become primary drivers of security spending for many organizations, and significant secondary drivers for most others. It's impossible to look at data security in a meaningful way without taking these regulatory issues into account. Let's begin, though, by looking briefly at the costs that can be associated with each of these nontechnological costs.

Design, Implement, and Manage

What does it cost to make security happen? This is a question that is difficult to answer with any certainty because commercial organizations are notoriously reluctant to release details on their security spending out of a fear that the information will be useful to criminals, industrial spies, and competitors. The US Federal Government does release such numbers, and the most recent information at the time of this writing provides an idea of the size of the investment the nation is prepared to make.

According to the budget proposal for fiscal 2013, the Obama administration requested $769 million for the National Cyber Security Division, a unit of government tasked solely with protecting governmental data resources.[1] This represents only a portion of the overall government spending on security. In an article published on Wired.com, Brito and Watkins point out that the Department of Defense requested more than $3.32 billion in fiscal 2012, and that analysts estimate that the federal government as a whole will request more than $10.5 billion for cyber security by 2015.[2] According to the current administration, the President's Budget for FY 2019 includes $15 billion of budget authority for cybersecurity-related activities, a $583.4 million (4.1 percent) increase above the FY 2018 estimate, although the statement on the request notes that this amount does not represent total cybersecurity spending, given the classified nature of some significant part of that activity (https://www.whitehouse.gov/wp-content/uploads/2018/02/ap_21_cyber_security-fy2019.pdf).

Although it is only so useful to compare the expenditures of the public sector to those of business, the numbers do emphasize an important point: The cost of designing, deploying, and managing a security infrastructure will be the most significant part of the total cyber-security budget. Because much of this expense will be ongoing, it's worth mentioning an advantage some organizations find in shifting security from the traditional, self-hosted model to a cloud architecture.

When organizations buy equipment such as firewall or UTM appliances, the funds most often come from the capital expense budget, generally referred to as "CAPEX" in conversation. Ongoing fees, such as those paid to cloud service providers, are operating expenses, called "OPEX" by those discussing such things. The key difference between CAPEX and OPEX, as shown in Figure 5.1, is in how the two are treated by tax codes, and what that difference in treatment means for the company's bottom line.

CAPEX is intended to provide a benefit that extends into the future for an organization. In the industrial age, heavy machinery and buildings fell into the capital expense category. Because of the future-looking nature of the expense, the cost can't be fully deducted from income in the year the expense occurs. The concepts of depreciation and amortization were created to account for CAPEX. OPEX is altogether different.

Operating expenses are just that: expenses incurred in the day-to-day operation of the business. Utility bills and lease payments are examples of operating expenses, and since the entire benefit of the expense is assumed to be immediate, OPEX is fully deductible in the year the payment is made. From an income tax point of view, the maximum deduction allowed for OPEX can be an important advantage. For companies trying to maximize their profitability, CAPEX may be preferred. The real point is that, for an expense that may be considerable for any company, technology may well be only one of the factors to be considered in the deployment decision. Another critical nontechnological factor is the ability to prove compliance with regulations and laws in security matters.

	Capital Expenditures	Operating Expenditures
Common Name	CAPEX	OPEX
Definition	Money spent for the future. The benefit to the business will come in the future, not in the same period as the expense.	Money spent in the day-to-day operation of the business. The benefit to the business is immediate.
Examples	Most equipment, significant infrastructure hardware, and large appliances.	Maintenance, leases, rentals, and licensing fees. Employee expenses.
Accounting Impact	The full deduction doesn't come in the same time frame as the expense. Depending on the asset, the expense may be either amortized or depreciated.	The expense is deducted in the same period as the expenditure. The accounting impact doesn't extend beyond the period of the expense.

Figure 5.1. CAPEX compared to OPEX.

The Cost of Compliance

There are few numbers about which you should have a more skeptical attitude than those regarding the cost of regulatory compliance. In many cases, numbers are produced by those with political points of view to advance. With that as prelude, let's talk about some compliance cost numbers.

According to the US Small Business Administration (SBA), the average cost to meet overall government regulations is $5,633 per employee. The cost of meeting economic regulations—those most likely to contain data security requirements—is estimated at $2,567 per employee.[3] It's notable that the study found that the per-employee cost of overall economic regulation compliance increased as the size of the company increased, from $2,127 to $2,952, as shows in Figure 5.2. Some of this is undoubtedly due to additional regulations that larger companies are subject to, but there's no question that compliance isn't free. It's also important to understand the costs not accounted for in the report.

The report's author notes that the methodology used only attempts to account for "first order" costs, those directly charged to compliance

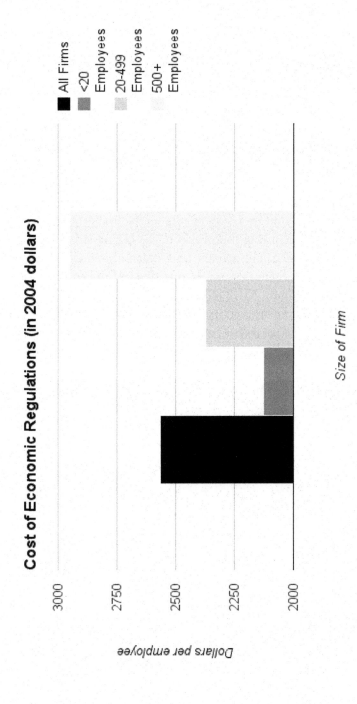

Figure 5.2. Company size compared to regulation cost.

efforts. Second order costs, those incurred as a result of compliance, are more difficult to measure with precision. In data security terms, those costs would be tied to issues such as reduced network throughput or increased help desk calls to deal with security-related issues. A more direct look at the costs of IT security comes through a report by the Ponemon Institute.

According to Ponemon, the average cost of compliance across a 46-company sample drawn from a number of different industries and organizational profiles, was $3,529,570.[4] Although an interesting number, for our purposes the more important number comes in a drill-down chart in which Ponemon breaks down the overall cost into six categories: Policy, Communications, Program Management, Data Security, Compliance Monitoring, and Enforcement. Four of these have a direct tie to the IT department, and their costs make up the lion's share of the total.

Data security is, according to Ponemon, the largest single contributor to the cost of compliance. The average organization spends $1,034,148 to achieve and prove data security, nearly one third of the total compliance cost, as indicated in Figure 5.3. Policy developing, establishing, and publishing the policy that ensures compliance with the relevant regulations is the smallest part of the total cost, accounting for an average of $297,910 to organizations. Compliance monitoring and enforcement together total slightly more than the cost of data security—$1,412,533—with compliance monitoring responsible for $636,542 and enforcement accounting for $775,991 of the total.

It's important to note that these are not one-time costs. These are the average costs for one fiscal year of regulatory compliance. When broken

Activity	Total	Average	Median
Policy	13,703,854	297,910	148,675
Data Security	47,570,815	1,034,148	793,352
Compliance Monitoring	29,280,953	636,542	326,181
Enforcement	35,695,589	775,991	266,753
Total	162,360,207	3,529,570	2,023,111

Figure 5.3. Compliance cost components (in US dollars). (*Source:* Ponemon Institute)

out by areas of function within the organization, Ponemon says that corporate IT is responsible for $1,073,720 of the overall cost, once again accounting for nearly one third of the company's total expenditure on regulatory compliance.

Before we leave the exploration of security costs, it's worth taking note of one more component of the total price tag. In slicing and dicing their way through their study results, the analysts at Ponemon found that specialized hardware accounts for an average of $923,917 of the total. This is an amount that approaches one third of the total cost of compliance, and will provide a great deal of the fodder for future discussion of the rationale behind much of the enterprise interest in cloud computing. Remember a few paragraphs back when we mentioned CAPEX and OPEX? Here are nearly a million reasons why that discussion was important.

From an accounting point of view, compliance as a whole represents money that contributes absolutely nothing to the core business of the enterprise. Moreover, an expenditure of nearly a million dollars (and keep in mind that this is an annual expense, not a one-time purchase) represents a significant addition to the "burden" that IT places on the balance sheet in the most optimistic analysis. While you're currently near the front of more than 200 pages of discussion about the technology and strategy of security involving the cloud, there are organizations for which the OPEX versus CAPEX comparison will trump all else. If you're part of one of these organizations, then our recommendation is to sharpen your spreadsheet skills and sally forth.

All of these factors together: policies, procedures, education, infrastructure, staffing, and compliance assurance, make up the price of data security, whether that security involves traditional data centers, cloud computing, or both. We now have a keen understanding that the price of security is likely to be high. It must be weighed, however, against the cost of security failures.

The Cost of Failure

A list of the worst data security breaches of the early part of this century is the stuff of Chief Information Security Officer (CISO) nightmares and the source for Figure 5.4. The least significant incident in a 2011 list published by *CSO Magazine* features more than 3.2 million records stolen

Number of Records Affected

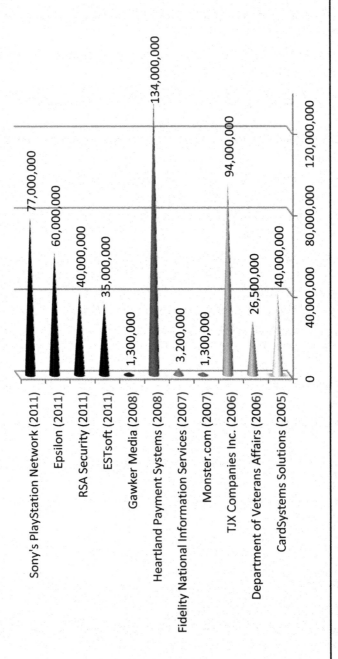

Figure 5.4. Significant data breaches of the last decade.

from Fidelity National Information Services in 2007.[5] The cost of this least-significant breach? A $3.2 million fine and a potential civil liability in excess of $64 million. Although there are certainly organizations that might consider a financial liability approaching $70 million to be insignificant, the authors consider such organizations to be members of a rather limited minority.

At the upper end of that list was the 2008 compromise of 134 million credit cards via an attack on Heartland Payment Systems. Although the financial repercussions to Heartland are still being determined some four years after the fact, the known costs are quite large. In a 2010 article on ComputerWorld.com, Jaikumar Vijayen reported that the costs were nearly $140 million dollars—a figure almost certainly to have increased since the article was published.[6] Although that is not the most expensive breach on record (that mark being held by the TJX exploit in 2006), it is yet another example of the sort of consequences that can apply when security fails.

In this same article, Vijayen quotes a Ponemon Institute report that the average cost of a US computer security breach was $6.75 million in 2009. It is reasonable to assume that this cost has risen (along with the cost of most things) in the years since that report. It is also reasonable to assume that this figure, while specific to the United States, is representative of similar costs in other jurisdictions. The European Union, in particular, has shown a tendency to take security breaches resulting in privacy violations very seriously—and "very seriously" translates quite rapidly into "very expensively" for the companies found to be in violation of regulations.

While these consequences are notable, it's important to note that there are other, also considerable, costs that can accrue through simply failing to comply with regulations and laws.

In the previously cited report on the cost of compliance,[4] the Ponemon Institute also calculated the cost of noncompliance, as shown in Figure 5.5. On average, Ponemon found that noncompliance costs an organization $9,368,351, which is more than two and a half times the cost of compliance. In a most interesting turn, they determined that the fines and regulatory penalties already discussed are among the smaller components in the overall cost. The largest portions of the total represent business disruption and productivity losses—factors that may be difficult to precisely calculate but are critical when understanding the true cost of failing to pay sufficient attention to the critical issues of regulatory compliance.

Consequence Costs	Average	Median	Maximum
Business Disruption	3,297,633	2,432,126	16,552,877
Productivity Loss	2,437,795	2,324,717	6,446,758
Revenue Loss	2,180,976	1,983,464	6,538,555
Fines, Penalties & Other	1,451,947	1,075,627	7,493,699
Total	9,368,351	9,336,084	27,974,560

Figure 5.5. Noncompliance cost details. (*Source*: Ponemon Institute)

Where Price and Consequence Intersect

Because no organization has an unlimited budget for security, each must figure out where the cost of security and the cost of data loss intersect (see Figure 5.6). This will be a unique point for each organization, but it does exist. At some levels, it's a very basic calculation, though arriving at the factors for the calculation can be anything but basic, as we've seen in the two previous sections.

We've talked about the costs of breaches, of noncompliance, and of the various forms of negative consequences that result from a security

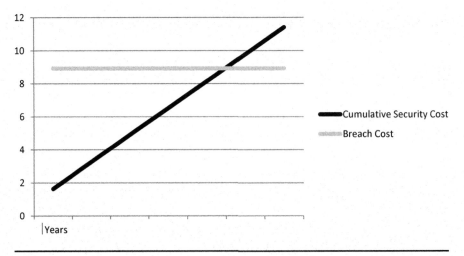

Figure 5.6. Intersecting security cost/breach cost lines.

breach, but here's the problem with providing these costs to the executive committee: These costs are not certain. There is no mathematical certainty that a given company will be the victim of a security breach in a given year. Regulatory compliance is somewhat more certain, since compliance must be audited and confirmed on a scheduled basis, but the large (and very public) costs of a breach might or might not happen.

The possibility of a year (or more) without breach leads some business leaders to wonder whether an element of risk is acceptable—whether gambling on both the possibility of a nonoccurrence and the scale of any breach might make it smarter to simply spend less on security and compliance than the prophets of doom in the IT department might deem ideal. They might just as well ask whether it's smarter to keep their home without homeowner's insurance. The real question is just how significant the consequences of The Worst Case Scenario might be.

Let's take a quick look at the consequences that faced Heartland Payment Systems after their notable breach in 2008. We've already seen the sort of direct financial costs associated with the breach, but there were other, still dramatic, effects from the loss of data integrity. One of the most significant was the loss of PCI certification that resulted from the specifics of the breach (a SQL Injection attack)—a loss that prevented the company from immediately resuming their primary business of clearing credit card transactions through the financial system. The lost revenue resulting from this business halt was nontrivial, and even when the certification was renewed, there was a lingering effect on consumer confidence in the security of credit card transactions.

Our financial systems run, to a great extent, on trust. When a company such as Heartland is compromised, it diminishes that trust. When that compromise occurs through a mechanism seen by many in the security community as "basic" as an SQL injection, the trust is diminished even farther. How many years of enhanced security expenses would have been justified if both the direct and indirect costs of the breach could have been avoided? That's the sort of question that organizations must answer when evaluating the appropriate level of security spending.

To properly evaluate the potential cost of a security failure, an organization must take into account not only the direct costs of data theft but all the indirect costs as well. From distraction and lost employee productivity to lost goodwill and opportunity costs, each of these must be accounted for if any sort of rational decision is possible. Now, the critical thing to keep in mind is that this is not an operation that can be completed by IT acting alone. Every department of the organization must be involved if costs are to be accurately assessed. Is this a monumental effort? Of course. For better or for worse, though, the importance of data and the severity of response when data integrity is breached justifies such a monumental operation.

The process of figuring out how expensive a data breach might be will, in itself, be expensive. Without going through this effort, though, an organization will almost certainly either leave itself open to risk that is demonstrably unacceptable, or commit resources to security that could more profitably be invested elsewhere. Take the time to figure it out. . . . Then you can begin the process of deciding how to keep the cost of security on the right side of the line you've drawn.

Stay on the Good Side of the Intersection

Once an organization has determined what it should be investing in security, it's time to implement. As we noted at the beginning of this chapter, implementation involves far more than just hardware purchase, and this is the point at which traditional security, cloud-based security, or (in a likely scenario) some combination of the two will be chosen. In addition to the financial considerations already discussed, today's organizations will engage in a conversation around competencies and which company should hold which competency as part of the decision-making process.

We have entered into one of the periodic swings to the "core competency" part of the business activity cycle. What is this cycle? There is a periodicity to the competing notions that businesses should own and control all the functions required for their business, on the one hand, and that businesses should understand their core competencies, focus only on those, and buy or outsource every other function, on the other hand. The rise of the cloud model of computing has given new life to the notion that many functions can be provided by partners, allowing the organization to focus on its core competencies.

Cloud computing allows for certain portions of the security infrastructure to be moved from the traditional capital-intensive, staff-intensive, company-controlled model to one in which a function is delivered in a pay-for-service business arrangement. Email security, both outbound and inbound, is one of the functions that many companies have moved into cloud implementation. Malware protection is another. Each of these can work through a proxy-type mechanism in which a cloud-based server relays all traffic of a specific type through a security mechanism before delivering it to the organization. Cloud architectures work well for services with nearly ubiquitous application (email is a key example of this sort of function) because mobile, modern organizations require a security application no matter where employees may be working from, especially when they are at locations far beyond the easy reach of data center-based services.

Of course, moving to the cloud is not without its own set of issues. As we saw earlier in this chapter, verifying and proving compliance with regulations is critical to security, and proving institutional control over services not owned by the institution is still, in some situations, being sorted out by both service provider and service customer organizations. The challenge of the core competency model is maintaining the proper level of institutional control over functions that might not be core, but are still critical. Security certainly falls within this sphere of activity, and organizations must find a balance between in-house and outsourcing, rigid control, and trust relationships. Those balances will be discussed in much more detail in later chapters.

References

1. "Fiscal Year 2013 Budget of the US Government." (2013). Retrieved from http://www.whitehouse.gov/sites/default/files/omb/budget/fy2013/assets/budget.pdf
2. Brito, J. and Watkins, T. (2012). "Wired Opinion: Cyberwar Is the New Yellowcake." *Wired*. Retrieved from http://www.wired.com/threatlevel/2012/02/yellowcake-and-cyberwar/
3. Crain, W. M. (2005). "The Impact of Regulatory Costs on Small Firms." United States Small Business Administration, under contract SBHQ-03-M-0522. Retrieved from http://archive.sba.gov/advo/research/rs264tot.pdf
4. Research Report Conducted by the Ponemon Institute, LLC. (2011, Jan.). "The True Cost of Compliance." Ponemon Institute, LLC.
5. Armerding, T. (2012, Feb. 15). "The 15 Worst Data Security Breaches of the 21st Century." CSO Online. Retrieved from http://www.csoonline.com/article/700263/the-15-worst-data-security-breaches-of-the-21st-century
6. Jijayen, J. (2010, May 10). "Heartland Breach Expenses Pegged at $140M, So far." *Computerworld*. Retrieved from http://www.computerworld.com/s/article/9176507/Heartland_breach_expenses_pegged_at_140M_so_far

Chapter 6

Defining the Cloud to Protect

A Very Quick Cloud Primer

We really can't stress enough that the science fiction world of being able to toss apps into the nebulous world of *the NET** without really caring what the underlying platform or operating system is, well, at the moment still science fiction. However, our working definition is that the cloud provides a way to disconnect you from the underlying hardware and physicality of running a traditional data center.

Just the concept of not having to worry about whether your app will run on the latest and greatest CPU chipset alone is making it worth looking into clouds. Legacy apps no longer have to mean legacy hardware.

The movement with the biggest promise of disconnecting us from needing to know about the underlying hardware layer is being done in

---

* Although not referencing any single title, "the NET" has come to describe some sort of nebulous service available to anyone willing to pay for it. Authors such as Arthur C. Clarke, Ray Bradbury, and Isaac Asimov have all made allusions to what sounds more like a utility than anything else. The point being that you just ask your question without regard to underlying operating system, architecture, or even native language.

the world of OpenStack® and the related software-defined networking (SDN). The baseline is that the world should eventually have to care less about the hardware and concentrate more on the tasks at hand. SDN currently has a groundswell of support from major players such as HP, Dell,™ IBM®, Netgear, and most of the major networking players in that demonstrations like those done by the iLabs group at the Interop™ Trade show have been showing how a heterogeneous collection of networking devices can be managed as a single entity. As an example, a short-term goal is to be able to manage dozens of workgroup switches across a multitude of physical locations as a single switch. So instead of a hundred 24-port switches, the entity acts as a single 2,400-port switch that can have services spread across the entity without regard to the physical location. To be more specific, a common example is forcing iPads/tablets into a single logical collection so that rules on the handling of these mobile devices are applied across the enterprise without the need to know exactly where those devices connect in.

Here is where we take a little bit of a side trip and start talking about clouds that start sounding like science fiction. The OpenStack.org folks are working toward removing the specificity of current virtualization offerings, with Rackspace.com one of the band leaders. At the current time, virtual servers come in a VMware® flavor or a Microsoft® flavor, but what some really want is another layer of abstraction that concentrates on getting the job done, rather than branding. The key to where clouds need to go is through provisioning applications or suites of applications for a task rather than getting caught up in the details of virtual machines. From an enterprise IT point of view, administrators would rather ask the cloud to set up an enterprise resource planning (ERP) system rather than having to define which virtual servers, with what kinds of resources and network connectivity, are needed to deploy that same ERP system. Microsoft's System Center 2016 and VMware's vSphere® 6.x vCloud Director already do this, but the system has to be defined at creation as a Microsoft or VMware flavor.

OpenStack.org is best described right now as a strong wish with enough pieces standing to bring a system up. However, the promise of OpenStack and OpenFlow® together make for a system such as that shown in Figure 6.1, where network, compute, storage, identity management, instance management, and systems control work in harmony, regardless of the underlying infrastructure. Notably, the hypervisor

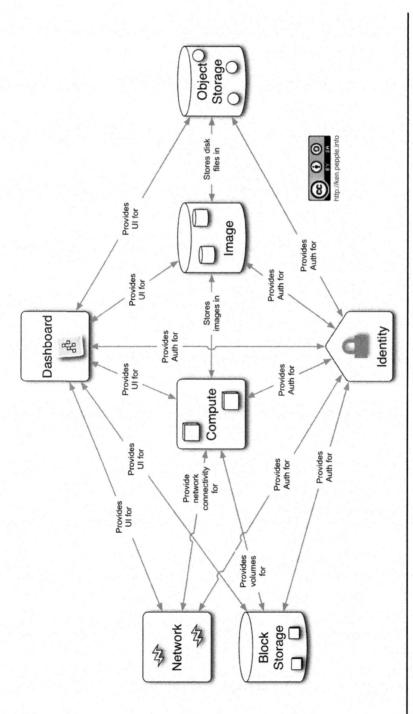

Figure 6.1. OpenStack conceptual architecture by Ken Pepple. Unlike traditional virtualization, OpenStack seeks to integrate the pieces together into a single entity and move towards provisioning "instances" instead of pieces. (Source: www.ken.pepple.info)

component supports the following at the time of this writing: RedHat®
KVM, Microsoft® Hyper-V®, VMware ESX®, Citrix® XenServer®, IBM®
Power VM®, and RedHat® Qemu.

> *The OpenStack project as a whole is designed to deliver a massively
> scalable cloud operating system. To achieve this, each of the constituent
> services are designed to work together to provide a complete
> Infrastructure as a Service (IaaS). This integration is facilitated
> through public application programming interfaces (APIs) that each
> service offers (and in turn can consume). While these APIs allow each
> of the services to use another service, it also allows an implementer
> to switch out any service as long as they maintain the API. These are
> (mostly) the same APIs that are available to end users of the cloud.*

> (*Source:* http://docs.openstack.org/trunk/openstack-compute/
> admin/content/conceptual-architecture.html)

What makes this movement so important is the promise that these
network entities no longer have to be in a single physical location but
should someday be able to extend into both public and private clouds.
The OpenStack (www.openstack.org) movement has been making
a plethora of promises that are being pushed by organizations such as
Rackspace.com and NASA, with the goal of creating a framework for
both public and private clouds that no longer rely upon vendor-specific
features or tools.

Although the exact relationship between SDNs, a.k.a. OpenFlow, and
the OpenStack world is nebulous, it's pretty obvious that you need to talk
about both in any conversation about the future of cloud computing.

Instance Provisioning Wins

Users have begun flocking to "virtual appliance" download sites to take
various systems for a test drive. The biggest challenges with this come
from complex systems such as Microsoft Skype for Business, which
require several interwoven Microsoft products in order to demonstrate
their full capability. Instead of investing huge sums of money in consulting services, Microsoft has instead created a downloadable array of virtual

machines that can be run as a complete system to help avoid common setup mistakes.

Just like many other complex products, demonstrations have always been a huge gamble for vendors due to the huge variability in demo infrastructure, and skill sets of those setting up the demo systems. Reviewer's guides have long been the bread and butter of these systems, with varying levels of success as users find new and unique ways to throw a monkey wrench into the demo works. What virtualization and, now, clouds give is the ability to drop into a virtualized environment a completely setup and tuned demonstration system. The key here is to build a single "perfect" demonstration system that's just flexible enough so that potential adopters can see key pieces of functionality in the demo that apply to their usage case. The next step is to have entire systems of interrelated services installed into the cloud as a single entity to better reflect resource requirements for a production system. Packaging the cloud is the logical next step, as the ability to define multiple system dependencies creates methods for defining heterogeneous system relationships.

It's very clear that Microsoft likes the idea of provisioning entire systems (a.k.a. instances) instead of a bucket of pieces, with the introduction of the Microsoft System Center Virtual Machine (scVMM) Manager 2012 as a part of System Center 2012. The key feature here is that scVMM is now capable of provisioning collections of resources from preallocated resource pools. Here is a description of the management suite:

Scenario: Deploy a Private VMM Cloud

A private cloud is a cloud that is provisioned and managed on-premises by an organization. It's deployed using an organization's own hardware to leverage the advantages of a private cloud model.

You can use VMM to create and deploy private cloud components, and to manage access to the private cloud and the underlying physical resources. VMM provides the following benefits:

- **Self-service**—*Self-service admins can delegate management and usage of the private cloud, while having no knowledge of underlying physical resources. They don't have to ask the private cloud provider for administrative changes, except to request increased capacity and quotas as required.*

- **Opacity**—*Self-service admins don't need any knowledge of underlying physical resources.*
- **Resource pooling**—*Administrators can collect and present an aggregate set of resources, such as storage and networking resources. Resource usage is limited by the capacity of the private cloud and by user role quotas.*
- **Elasticity**—*Administrators can add resources to a private cloud to increase the capacity.*
- **Optimization**—*Usage of the underlying resources is continually optimized without affecting the overall private cloud user experience.*

You can create a private clouds from either:

- *VMM host groups that contain resources from virtualization hosts.*
- *A VMware resource pool*

You deploy a private cloud by configuring fabric resources, settings up library paths for private cloud users, and setting cloud capacity.

Source: https://docs.microsoft.com/en-us/system-center/vmm/deploy-cloud?view=sc-vmm-1801. Used with permission November 20, 2018.

Not to be left out, VMware's vCloud Director® provides similar capability and is described by VMware's advertisements, as follows:

Orchestrate the provisioning of software-defined datacenter services as complete virtual datacenters that are ready for consumption in a matter of minutes. Virtual datacenters provide virtualized compute, networking, storage, and security. Administrators can provision the complete set of services necessary to make workloads operational in minutes. Software-defined datacenter service and the virtual datacenters fundamentally simplify infrastructure provisioning, and enable IT to move at the speed of business.

(*Source:* http://www.vmware.com/products/vcloud-director/overview.html)

So whether you're using OpenStack, Microsoft, or VMware, it's all about being able to cookie cutter entire data centers or individual business lines (i.e., ERP, CRM, etc.) as an "instance," instead of getting lost in a massive checklist of moving parts.

Look at it as the progression of local area networks and how the industry started as discretely managed network workstations, to server-based systems administration, to directory forest (collection of workstations and servers) management, and now to federated connections between forests. It only makes sense that management aggregation also happens at the cloud level, and that enterprise policy is implemented at these same levels.

Survey the Cloud: Understand Protection

Ask any law enforcement officer about protection and you'll always get a question back asking you to define the scope of what are you trying to protect. The same goes for clouds, and your starting point really needs to be an inventory. The old writer's checklist of "Who, What, Where, When, and How" is wonderfully appropriate when creating a "scope of protection" for single systems or clouds.

Another good analogy, "How do you eat an elephant?" and "One bite at a time," is a great way to start. Ask your teams to apply the "Who, What, Where, When, and How" to define their systems, and your role is to collect the answers and look at the individual bites as a whole elephant again. Then apply those same questions to how each team's resources interact with one another, and all of a sudden you have the beginning of a "chart of relationships" that's a terrific starting point for your security audit.

Let's add a bit more detail to the "Who, What, Where, When, and How" questions and apply them to both public and private clouds, by starting off with a suggested checklist:

- **Who** is using the system. Go beyond just a list of employees; go further into organizational roles and what groups they touch, and then define how their roles touch other roles.
- **What** resources, applications, data stores, etc., do they need to get to. Locking things up and throwing away the key is only whimsy, and to do business there are always going to be compromises. What are those compromises?

- **Where** are all those resources? Have you outsourced pieces? Do some of your pieces live with partners? Also WHERE are those agreements for access to external resources?
- **When** do your people need access? Are your operations round the clock? Do you need to limit access to certain times? Are those limitations in different time zones? Do holidays affect access rules?
- **How** do you limit access? In the old days of mainframes, CICS had limitations imposed by the 3270 terminal address. Do you need to lock things down so that something supersensitive (say international banking funds transfer) can only be done from certain physical machines AND require multiple layers of biometric and password authentication from different people, depending upon who you're going to transfer money to and how much money.

Let's get back to that elephant. A favored method is to push every business unit to answer these questions for internal versus external users. They should also consider quantifying how roles within their department/division/etc. should have differing access, and whether those rules are native to your organization or are driven by regulations. This should all sound very familiar and something that you might have wanted to do for a long time. Go ahead. Use clouds as an excuse to play catch-up. And catch up you MUST do, since now some of your enterprise is out of sight and mind. Just the act of writing it down can be of significant value, and an exercise worth doing as an organization, just as strategic planning typically has the entire organization build a new goal statement. This exercise just means you're on the same page.

Next, what has already been outsourced and where are those service level agreements (SLAs)? Securing any sort of public cloud means you need to understand what your service provider is willing to do and what they are bound by contract to do. You also need to review that agreement and ask if remediation is worth your human resource cost or whether it's best to just make sure you have an alternate source of recovery. Something along the line of maybe it's cheaper to fix that broken window yourself after that windstorm than submitting an insurance claim that would raise your rates. Review that SLA and ask yourself if the demands you've made of the service provider are really worth pursuing, and do this review at reasonable intervals. Maybe a new technology is going to make it way cheaper to execute the recovery yourself, instead of depending upon an expensive service from the provider.

Ask anyone responsible for dealing with classified computer data and they'll tell you that it's the day-to-day auditing that drives them to drink. Sifting through thousands of log entries per hour generated by a modern IT system just won't get done, and even if you force someone to do it, their eyes are going to glaze over, and in no time they're not even going to recognize their own name much less a security event. The key here is to let computers do what they're good at and that's unblinking attention to detail 24×7×365, all without holidays or breaks. The key here is automating the odious tasks, but verifying that they're working. We'd also like to point out that no matter what the sales people tell you, we've never found a single monitoring/auditing system that does it all. Here is a great place to say that "defense in depth" makes a whole lot of sense because software, like all human endeavors, is prone to errors, and it just makes sense to make sure your systems have at least a little bit of overlap.

Protection Depends on the Cloud

If everything you have in the cloud is public information and doesn't contain any personally identifying information, then perhaps you don't need to apply as many layers of defense. However, if you have patient/financial/etc. information with a bunch of government regulations, then maybe those extra layers are worth the time and money.

Go back to the "Who, What, Where, When, and How" questions and take a good hard look at measuring your risk. You might also want to ask yourself if the cloud is gathering information to bring inside your company's firewalls, and consider some sort of DMZ vault as a first stop— someplace to put the data under a microscope of malware scanners to make sure you're not bringing a Trojan horse into the city walls.

Let's also make sure you measure the risk about whether you really need to extend your organization's identity management system [i.e., Lightweight Directory Access Protocol (LDAP) or Active Directory (AD)] into the cloud, or will a read-only copy suffice? We've even been hearing about some organizations treating their cloud facilities like an external organization and using federated authentication for their cloud facilities. Keep in mind that it might not be a great idea to put a full backup copy of your AD schema into a public cloud, and that you may want to thin it down, anyway, to use less-chargeable resources from that public cloud vendor.

We certainly can't pretend that one size fits all in the world of clouds, regardless of whether you're using a private cloud or public cloud; it's all about making sure that you NEVER forget that this cloud facility isn't inside the organization walls, and applying even a little bit of paranoia couldn't hurt. Just put on a black hat for a bit and look at what you have in the cloud. Here are a few common sense questions you might want to ask yourself during the planning process:

- Can you be hurt by someone getting hold of that data?
- Can you be hurt by someone falsifying data in that system?
- What are the ramifications if that data goes missing?
- What do you lose if the cloud services go away (e.g., during a natural disaster)?

This all sounds tedious, time consuming, and expensive. But how much will it cost your organization if the answer to any of these questions become true? Use the move to the clouds as your excuse to do it right, and really embrace the changes you're thinking about implementing. Everyone who we've spoken to about a move into the clouds has opinions about a rainbow of cautionary tales; however, they all seem to agree that going slowly and documenting the entire process has and always will pay dividends in the long run.

Chapter 7

Infrastructure as a Service

Outsourcing Equipment Used to Support Operations, Including Storage, Hardware, Servers, and Networking Components

There is often confusion when people try to understand the difference between Infrastructure as a Service (IaaS) and Platform as a Service (PaaS). It's an easy point for confusion since both layers sit below the applications and middleware services that many companies choose as their first points of entry to the cloud.

The easiest way to understand the differentiation is that a *platform* will run on top of the *infrastructure*. Phrased another way, the infrastructure is closer to the essential hardware than is the platform. Now, the reality is considerably messier than this because there is no standard set of industry terms for referring to either of these—they tend to be phrases of art or marketing as much as technical descriptions. In addition, in very many cases, a service provider might offer a set of services that would logically span both terms. Welcome to the cloud.

Be that as it may, in this chapter we're going to look at IaaS and how security is applied to this layer. In doing so, we'll be looking not only at

IaaS as a discrete layer in the overall application stack but also at all the different infrastructures that can be provided in the cloud model—infrastructures that include video, telephone, networking, and computing capabilities.

Let's first examine IaaS from the more "traditional" point of view—one that deals with an infrastructure that supports the sort of applications that most users think of when they imagine cloud computing. We'll see that each of the characteristics that make IaaS a compelling option for many enterprises also brings with it a set of risk factors that can lead to significant security issues for careless companies.

Utility Model—Pay for Time and Resources Used

One of the key characteristics of the IaaS model is that it mimics something with which we're all familiar: the public utilities delivering electricity, gas, and other basic physical infrastructure services. In those physical cases, the utility company invests in massive power generation or gas-processing equipment, but the customer only pays for the portion of the resulting products that they actually use. Only in rare cases (e.g., farms with only a single home in a large land area) will the utilities impose on the customer a portion of the cost to set up the service. But the analogy still works because even IaaS folks will make you share some of the costs if you ask for something far outside of their normal service offerings.

In IaaS, the cloud service provider buys and maintains a server farm larger than most enterprises would need on anything like a regular basis. The customers can purchase the use of the services provided by that server farm as they need them, and pay for them when needed. The economies work for both sides of the relationship.

Because IaaS operates at a "lower" level than the visible operating system, it is subject to threats that operating systems themselves aren't vulnerable to. One of the more intriguing and insidious of these threats is hyperjacking, replacing the hypervisor on which the virtualized servers run with a system controlled by an unauthorized individual.

As of the time of this writing, hyperjacking is a threat that has been proven in the lab but not seen in the wild. Nevertheless, it has occupied a great deal of server administrator attention since 2011. Fortunately, the problem is easily described and prevented through straightforward processes.

The Danger of the Hyperjack

In hyperjacking, the hypervisor itself is replaced by a compromised piece of software that allows the hijacked hypervisor's owner to control the operation of the operating system instances running on the hypervisor, the resources dedicated to the instances, and (potentially most important) the data processed in and transferred among the instances.

The critical danger in hyperjacking isn't so much that the operating system instances on a physical server could be compromised. No, the critical danger is that the compromise happens at a software level below the logical layer at which anti-malware and other security mechanisms operate. The danger is then amplified by the possibility that the server instances of scores (or hundreds) of customers could be compromised on a single physical server.

By now you should be getting an idea of why security professionals have taken the threat of hyperjacking seriously. There is good news, however, despite all the scary stuff. The good news begins with the fact, as already stated, that there has been no example of hyperjacking identified "in the wild." It's also true that hypervisors are not, by their nature, easy to reach. A rootkit targeting the hypervisor would have to be launched on a system employing a processor that allows untrusted program execution. Difficulty is no defense, however, and the active defenses against hyperjacking contain lessons for other protective measures.

Defense against Hyperjacking

With the possibility that the hypervisor (or even lower-execution levels) could be compromised, software and hardware companies alike realized that security required the ability to trust the basic units of computing on which virtual operating systems and clouds were built. The Trusted Computing Group (TCG), an industry standards organization founded in 2003, developed the Trusted Platform Module (TPM) as a way of ensuring a secure configuration for the computing infrastructure.

The TPM concept rests on a two-part process: Measure key aspects of the boot configuration, and only then proceed with system start. This delayed start is critical for ensuring the security of systems that might otherwise be subject to root kits and hyperjacking. Two factors—one variable and one fixed—make up the core of a TPM implementation.

Variation comes in what, precisely, is measured. It might be a configuration file, it might be the contents of the boot sector, or it could be a known portion of the BIOS. Whatever it is, the known-good state is captured, a secure hash algorithm applied (SHA-1 at the time of this writing), and the resulting number stored in a repository. At boot time, in a step before the operating system is loaded, the designated files are read, the hash algorithm run, and the result compared with the stored sum. Only if the two results match does booting continue. Of course, in its most effective implementation this requires the non-variable factor.

TPM becomes truly effective when it is supported by the CPU on which the system is built. Intel® has done just that with Trusted Execution Technology (TXT) in their Trusted Computing Pool products. TXT, part of the Intel Xeon® CPU line, delays completion of the boot process until the TPM sequence has been completed and the secure state of the system verified. This partnership of solid process, security-aware operating system, and process-supporting hardware can provide protection against hyperjacking—and a solid foundation for secure IaaS.

For customers of IaaS clouds, it provides another set of items on a security checklist that can help deliver the reasonable expectation of security. This will be reassuring when employee desktops, enterprise networks, unified communications, and other services are delivered through a cloud architecture. This assurance is especially important as more and more of the infrastructure is provided on a service model.

Desktop Virtualization

Although most enterprises have converted somewhere between "many" and "all" of their servers to virtual service, virtual desktops are much less common. There are, though, a number of reasons for the increasing popularity of virtual desktops. Those reasons are only amplified when the desktops are served from a cloud infrastructure.

There are, broadly speaking, two models for providing virtual desktops. In one, a master image of the desktop operating environment is used as the basis for each user's deployed operating system—deployed copies that may then be somewhat customized by the user and saved, so that the individualized operating system is available each time the user logs into the enterprise system. In the other, no such customization is possible: Each user is presented a uniform "vanilla" operating system at each invocation.

Regardless of the model, there are three benefits that just about every organization is looking for when they move to virtual desktops: simplified deployment, greater security, and reduced support costs. The cost and simplicity issues are beyond the scope of this book. The real question for us to examine here is whether—and how—virtual desktops are more or less secure than traditional desktop clients. The answer to the question, as with so much of life, is, "yes—and no."

Desktop virtualization is not, by itself, a magic potion that bestows instant security on an environment. Experts agree that poor traditional desktop security practices brought intact into a virtual environment result in an insecure virtual desktop installation.[1]

Desktop Virtualization Issues

The "greater security" piece of the benefit puzzle is open to some debate. As mentioned above, a virtualized desktop is not inherently secure, although there are some implementations that lack certain sets of vulnerabilities. Virtual desktops implemented on "zero clients" (client hardware that has no local memory, storage, or the ability to boot without connection to the virtual desktop server) are not vulnerable to attacks that begin with a breach of the client computer operating system.

Virtual desktops running as client software on fully functional endpoints (whether handheld mobile devices or laptop computers) are a different story—aren't they? Well, yes and no. The primary danger lies in the possibility that data might be transferred from the virtual desktop to the actual physical client and then lost. Fortunately for the enterprise IT department, solutions to the primary danger are straightforward, if not always simple.

Desktop Virtualization Defense

The first concern for most IT professionals is data in motion—the data that flows between devices. The primary defense for data in motion between virtual devices is the same as the defense for non-virtual systems:

a combination of strong authentication and encryption—encryption typically taking place through the mechanism of a virtual private network (VPN).

Network Virtualization

When all the resources that go into making a network—hardware, software, functions, processes, and services—are combined into a single logical entity for management and administration purposes, the foundation has been laid for network virtualization. The benefits of network virtualization lie in two major areas: management simplification and better resource utilization.

It's difficult to look at the precise benefits of network virtualization until you specify what type of network virtualization is being discussed. Both *internal* and *external* network virtualization are in use by various companies and organizations (along with hybrid forms blending the two), and each provides different functions for the purpose of providing different benefits.

Internal network virtualization always occurs in the company of server virtualization. In the case of internal network virtualization, each virtual server is provided with its own logical network address and set of network capabilities that are then mapped onto a traditional network at the physical server's network interface card (NIC). Each logical server therefore acts as though it has complete use and control of the physical network. In simple terms, internal network virtualization takes many virtual networks *inside* the physical server and maps them onto a single logical network *outside* the server.

Security can be improved for the applications running on the virtual server because the traffic from those applications can be isolated from the traffic of other virtual servers and protected as a separate data stream. Internal network virtualization reduces the chance that an exploit affecting one virtual server will be able to compromise the data streams of other virtual servers on the same physical platform. Performance of the overall network may be improved because the various virtual servers will be able to jointly make more efficient use of the NIC (or NICs) present in the physical server.

Virtual Network Issues

Keep in mind that nothing comes for free, and virtual network interface cards (vNICs) are no exception. You may find that your IaaS provider's default vNIC is a 100mb/sec generic, and to get gig or 10gig involves paying for higher service tiers. The same goes for the speed of your virtual switch, since they all take up a limited set of resources on the virtual host that soaks up power, cooling, and probably some sort of interest on a loan to pay for all of it.

This is a case in which you may want to find out if the IaaS vendor has some package deals. It might be called "Flavors" (Rackspace®) or service tiers by others; but these tiers all represent resource pools that can be draw against as you set up your virtual systems.

A word of caution: Find out during your sign-up what happens if you surge past your plan's limits. Do you have a grace period during which you can surge for a couple minutes, but if it drops down quickly, you don't get a huge overage charge, or worse, you hit a hard limit. Like cell phone providers, you're talking about their bread and butter, so make sure you know if there are any types of overage charges on your resource pool. You might find it's cheaper to go one tier higher if you keep hitting the plan's ceiling.

Virtual Network Defense

There have been lots of conversations about the "end of the perimeter" and those folks need to be reminded that unless you're able to run your servers wide open to the world; you're always going to have to protect the inside from the outside. The perimeter may no longer be an enterprise grade firewall separating the trusted from untrusted from the DMZ, but it still needs to exist. Where that edge/perimeter is depends upon who you talk to, Google® and Microsoft® both seem to be heading toward using some sort of gateway server in order to access organization resources. Microsoft calls it either a federation gateway or RDP gateway, but the gist is that you're connecting an encrypted pipe from the user endpoint to this gateway, and then after trust is confirmed, you forward the still encrypted connection to the true destination. The gateways may or may not contain a proxy, but it does give you a point at which to deeply examine the incoming traffic before you get to the trusted network(s).

We think the real conversation is about whether you stay with a VPN mesh between your locations and put your perimeter outside this mesh, or whether you draw a protected line to each workstation and consider anything not coming over that protected circuit to be "outside."

Storage Virtualization

So whereas folks at VMware® have been testing the waters with their VSphere® Storage Appliance™ (VSA), which seems to have a goal of reclaiming all the "wasted storage" on ESXi nodes, the real conversation is about inserting an additional layer of abstraction that allows for vendors to insert additional features without having to re-architect the entire system.

Features like de-duplication, array to array copy/move, and cross hardware volumes have advanced to the point where they've gone from cool new features to expected ones. At the 2012 Microsoft STB Reviewers Workshop, the world press had an unexpected feature announced about a growing number of network attached storage (NAS) appliances that can support SMB v3 AND the ability for Server 2012 R2 to directly mount these volumes for hypervisor images. This set the stage for a whole new series of SMB virtualization packages. More importantly, this means that in terms of IaaS applications, you might be able to move some of your less-critical systems to less-expensive (but slower) storage tiers.

Storage Network Issues

Which network you put your storage on becomes a matter for arguing best practices, and if you ask 10 people you'll more than likely get 10 different answers. However, one common thread is going to be lowering the latency and maximizing throughput between arrays and nodes.

Storage Network Defense

Here, the question is whether you commit to an airgap or mix it with the rest of the data center traffic. It's certainly cheaper to not request separate vSwitches for storage, but some thought should be given to how much access you want to give to storage traffic, especially when there is typically less in the way of checks and balances for storage networking connections. We also tend to think of storage traffic as needing low latency, especially for things such as databases. And to that end, we've seen quite a few sysadmins modify the maximum transmission unit (MTU)* optimized to the size of the average SQL query. From both an optimization and security standpoint, separating storage traffic from user traffic makes a lot of sense.

Just keep in mind that vSwitches do NOT have to be linked together, and that we've mostly seen storage vSwitches completely isolated from user vSwitches by using a second vNIC on the virtual server. As long as you don't turn on IP forwarding on your machines, the storage vSwitches can remain isolated.

Other Infrastructure Types

This is where we talk about services and infrastructure that just don't fit into any of the traditional categories. The first emerging technology that's blurring the lines has got to be software-defined networking (SDN), where we no longer have traditional VLANs/vSwitches/etc. but rather a truly cloudy network that supposedly can support a giant mix of packet sizes and types, which can appear at any or all of your edges. Microsoft has gone as far as integrating in border gateway protocol (BGP) so that entire domains can be terminated right at the server/gateway virtual machine. What really makes this technology blurry is how perimeters/boundaries/etc. aren't as well defined anymore, and whether your resources are in the cloud, local data center, or ISP no longer matters.

The other emerging technology that doesn't even have a recognized name yet is what we're calling "Workstation as a Service" (WaaS), where the virtualized workstation has access to some sort of graphics co-processor. Here the intent is to share an expensive graphics processing unit (GPU) (some now priced at many thousands of US dollars each) for hardware supported 3D rendering. Typical uses aren't for gaming but rather 3D CAD (i.e., AutoDesk® Revit®, Maya®, Renderman®, etc.) or scientific

---

* http://en.wikipedia.org/wiki/Maximum_transmission_unit

simulations such as BLAST® (genetics), MATLAB®, Mathematica®, etc. So although Microsoft's Server 2012 R2 now provides software-simulated GPUs, only hardware GPUs are viable for many science and engineering applications. The two major categories of shared GPUs are:

1. GPU Passthrough: This is where the entire GPU is dedicated to the virtual workstation for each shared time slice. So even if your workstation only needs a little bit of GPU to handle something as simple as "Aero Glass" in Windows® 8, it would get the entire GPU for its time slice. This setup (at the time of writing and is likely to change by the time this books is being sold) is typical of the VMware- and Citrix®-shared GPU solutions and only works for a small number of certified GPU boards. Even though Citrix virtual desktops (XenDesktop® and XenApp®) are supported with VMware or Microsoft Hyper-V® as a foundation, the shared GPU environment is ONLY available for Citrix XenServer®.
2. Shared GPU: Think of this like a game of Tetris®, where varying size blocks fit together to fill the volume of the system. In this case, as you provision your virtual workstations, you set a maximum number of monitors, monitor resolution, and color depth. This determines just how much video resources need to be pre-allocated to each virtual workstation. The Microsoft RemoteFX® system will then fit these requirements into the available GPU resources and service as many virtual workstations as possible with the available resources. So in the case of the Aero Glass interface, it might assign very little video RAM, whereas a user running AutoDesk 3D AutoCAD® would be assigned more. (*Note:* When we started writing this book, Citrix ONLY handled GPU passthrough, but early in 2014 they began offering a shared GPU solution similar to Microsoft's RemoteFX setup)

Unified Communications Clouds

The whole Unified Communications (UC) movement has floundered in the enterprise, while exploding in the public. The most common complaint we've heard about UC in general is that it breaks almost every single regulatory regime due to the lack of auditing and control capability. It's literally an all or nothing affair for just about all the popular

UC solutions (Skype®, Cisco Jabber®, FaceTime®, Facebook™ Messenger, Google Hangouts™, etc.), and we would imagine that those folks really don't want to be "compliant" due to the insane overhead costs of making audit trails available to investigators. So perhaps it's best for them to bury their heads in the sand and intentially not hold audit trails, so there is nothing for the legal folks to "discover."

However, UC in general is way too useful to be ignored by the regulated organizations to the point where there was a US Department of Defense (DoD) request for a proposal that required a system similar to what LinkedIn® has, but that had components for contact technologies that looked as if it would need to scale from email, to text, to voice, to video—basically a UC version of LinkedIn that would service the military. Obviously, there was a huge component on auditing and a huge rules database to determine who could contact whom and under what conditions. I nearly submitted a proposal (ran out of time) for a Microsoft Active Directory®–based system with SharePoint® and Lync®. The reality is that Microsoft has built in a huge collection of audit capabilities within Active Directory, which then controls how SharePoint, Exchange®, Lync, and Office® all handle who gets to contact and share with whom.

So more to the point, Microsoft is actually getting pretty close to being able to support what the DoD wanted, right out of the box. Office 365®, in the cloud now, has most of Lync and most of SharePoint, with Exchange as their email solution. The point is that there are quite a few UC systems starting to emerge that are based upon the Microsoft suite (think phone vendors adding UC to their telco solutions) mostly because the audit and business rule capabilities can fulfill even the most stringent of regulations. We're thinking that you'll be able to have a fully functional UC solution in public, private, or hybrid clouds by the time this book hits the shelves.

Physical Security Clouds

First and most importantly, physical security is no longer the world of laser cut keys and time locks on vaults. More and more physical security systems are being tied into the IT realm using Identity Management Systems so that the physical and virtual worlds can be cross-correlated. For example, here are two events:

1. Legitimate user authenticates into the corporate VPN gateway from overseas.
2. Legitimate user "scans" into secure areas in the physical plant.

What makes this scary is if these two events are for the same user! Each on its own is perfectly legitimate, but together should send security into fits immediately.

So as the physical and IT security databases grow, the same questions about whether to leave them on premise or go to the cloud rise to the surface. This is similar to the arguments about directory structures for network resource authentication (Active Directory, LDAP, NIS, etc.)—regarding whether you centralize the authentication, send it all to the cloud, or create some sort of hybrid arrangement. Similar arguments arise as to whether you shadow full copies of the information or set up read-only versions that sync periodically with the main image.

References

1. Wood, A. and Haletky, E. (2011, Dec.). "A VDI Desktop Is No More Secure Than a Standard Desktop." *The Virtualization Practice.* Retrieved from http://www. virtualizationpractice.com/a-vdi-desktop-is-no-more-secure-than-a-standard-desktop-13714/

Chapter 8

Platform as a Service (PaaS)

PaaS is a new label for virtualizing entire machines and systems. In our opinion, it's the self-service nature of the provisioning process that separates PaaS from traditional virtualization and the ability to provision a collection of resources such as virtual switches, databases, middleware, and front ends. So think an entire cake instead of just eggs, flour, sugar, and such.

A Way to Rent Hardware, Operating Systems, Storage, and Network Capacity Over the Internet

Let's face it: Data centers are a cost item—a BIG cost item—and building one for a short-term project is every CFO's nightmare. We've become all too familiar with the formula of *equipment_cost* + *power_cost* + *cooling_cost* + *maintenance* + *depreciation* = *OMG really?* There have been a plethora of schemes devised to avoid CFO involvement in the equipment purchase by shuffling cost centers once the project is done:

- eBay®
- Donate it to a school or charity.
- Persuade another department to take over the facility.

- Persuade the CFO that you really need to expand your regular data center
- Move it into a colocation facility and hope to hide it from the CFO
- Turn out the lights and lock the door in the hope that no one will notice

One possible solution is renting or leasing the equipment for the project, but we still need to deal with the cost of the floor space, power, cooling, and lease/rent agreement. This is better, but someone needs to make a profit on the rental, and you're still paying for the depreciation but now it's buried in the rental cost. You're now also fighting with the facilities group because you've shifted the cost of power and cooling to them. What is a project manager to do?

What the industry needed was a way to be able to walk away once the project was done and to keep the costs predictable. Although by no means the first, our favorite example involves *The New York Times* and Amazon™ combining forces to set the industry on end with a paradigm shift. The scenario involved is one in which *The New York Times* had already scanned their entire back issue collection but had not yet indexed it. The problem the project leader faced was how to amass enough computing power to do the indexing without creating a white elephant that their department would have to pay for over coming fiscal years. The answer it seemed was a new service being offered by Amazon called their Elastic Compute Cloud™ or EC2™.

A great example of how the Amazon EC2 system has been used in the past is an industry story of how *The New York Times* had a problem regarding how to index a massive number of scanned back copies of the publication. The goal was to take these scanned images and to index them and add them to the searchable index of *The Times*.

So, although the number of virtual machines used for this task varies with each telling of this story, the bottom line is that *The Times* was able to rent a significant number of virtual machines in the Amazon EC2 cloud, run the indexing, and then walk away. What makes this so significant is that *The Times* did NOT have to purchase, setup, house, and maintain a larger number of servers for a one-time project. Rumor has it that the cost to rent those virtual machines was actually less than the estimated maintenance cost of a similar system.

The point is that the project lead quite literally rented a couple of thousand machines that were all running the indexing software, thereby churning out the back issue indexing project in a weekend, and then walked away once it was done. Well, he probably kept a copy of the "gold image" on file so that it could be easily duplicated later, but the world of on-demand computing had begun. And the rent on those virtual machines was probably less than just the maintenance cost on the machine they would have had to purchase in past years.

However, Amazon is far from being the only game in town, and cloud computing service providers have started popping up like mushrooms. Additional major players include Google®, Microsoft®, and IBM®, with scores of smaller, more specialized operators also entering the market. With the growing vendor population, the industry became quite confusing, with the number of cloud flavors nearly equaling the number of providers. With VMware®-, Microsoft-, and Linux®-based clouds to choose from, customers currently have to choose one technology on which to bet; however, the Open Source world is riding to the rescue with the previously mentioned (see Chapter 6) OpenStack® project providing a greater level of abstraction in order to remove the need to choose between the foundational hypervisor systems.

What needs to be pointed out is that this kind of cloud computing works fine for line-of-business applications but has been disappointing, so far, for high-performance computing (HPC) installations ("supercomputing clusters" running under Beowulf technology [http://en.wikipedia. org/wiki/High-performance_computing]) because the extra overhead of the hypervisor soaks away performance with the overhead load intrinsic to cloud management.

Systems Can Be Used to Run Service-Provided Software, Packaged Software, or Customer-Developed Software

As journalists, we receive emails, conduct interviews, and read many surveys about what our readers or viewers really want. The bottom line is that users don't want to worry about running a data center; they want to use it and forget about the details. That's the promise of clouds and why we're

Figure 8.1. Grace Murray Hopper at the UNIVAC® keyboard, c. 1960. Rear Admiral Hopper was an American mathematician and rear admiral in the US Navy, and she was a pioneer in developing computer technology, helping to devise UNIVAC I, one of the first commercial electronic computers and naval applications for COBOL (COmmon-Business-Oriented Language). (*Source:* http://en.wikipedia.org/wiki/Grace_hopper)

seeing a trend towards clouds that many journalists have been describing as a "swing back towards mainframes." We keep harping on how cloud computing exemplified the way science fiction is turning into science fact. But it's not the remote computing that's caught people's imaginations; it's the ability to take "off-the-shelf software" and be able to scale it up to handle massive tasks. These same people are imagining something as easy to use as a spreadsheet but able to handle petabytes of data coming from thousands of sources. A good example is how marketing agencies would love to be able to harvest data coming from government agencies all over the world [through something like the "open government" or "open data" movements occurring all over the United States (http://en.wikipedia.org/wiki/Open_data)] and correlate that data with private marketing data to come up with ever more targeted sales pitches. The variability of this kind of question makes an in-house system either limited or insanely expensive; it would be much better to let this kind of surge need be handled by a service where you just pay as you go.

Analysts need only look at trends in computer language complexities to see the writing on the wall. Pioneers such as Grace Hopper (see Figure 8.1;

the inventor* of COBOL [http://en.wikipedia.org/wiki/Grace_hopper])
grew up in a world that required glass rooms and specialists in white
lab coats tending to the temples of computing. However, Rear Admiral
Hopper started us down the road toward being able to avoid machine
language programming gibberish and start using human languages to
tell computers what to do. As the industry grew up, more and more
specialized computer languages were developed to make interactions with
computers more and more humanlike. We're certainly seeing that in voice
command systems such as Apple®'s Siri®, Amazon's Alexa®, and Google's
voice command (an integral part of Google Glass™), as well as Google
Translate™ (http://googletranslate.blogspot.com/#googtrans/en/en). And
we're most certainly seeing it in systems such as Dragon® Dictate and
Window®'s voice command.

As clouds grow and the market makes increasing demands on the
developers, we're sure we'll see more computing systems based upon
human interfaces such as touch, voice, and biometrics. Just look at the
media hype behind Google Glass to get a glimpse of this market demand
and Google Glass's subsequent collapse when market expectations far
exceeded reality when the product finally shipped to consumers. At the
same time, machine-to-machine communications have become standardized to the point where it has started to become commonplace for home
appliances to have programming interfaces for integration into larger
systems. Probably the best examples of this are photovoltaic power generation systems: Customers now demand the ability to remotely see the
power production and health of their systems. It is exciting that systems
like those developed by SMA-America (Sunny Boy® inverters and Sunny
WebBoxes®) not only push data up to a power-production tracking cloud
but also have a full set of FTP push, json, and csv capabilities, along with
APIs (http://en.wikipedia.org/wiki/API) and SDKs (http://en.wikipedia.
org/wiki/Software_development_kit) for harvesting data off the system
(http://www.sma.de/en/products/monitoring-systems/sunny-webbox.

---

* Grace Hopper is considered the mother of COBOL, but, as in any giant project, no
  one person could have written it in all. Nonetheless, she is considered the author of
  modern COBOL. Brian was honored to have been able to attend a lecture by then
  Commander Grace Hopper, and, yes, she ALWAYS credits a team effort. However, the
  admirals of the time have credited her as being the original author.

html). (*Note:* The industry is finally seeking a standard. The preliminary name for this is SunSpec®, and the goal is to enable power utilities to remotely "power back" home inverters to prevent overloading the local grid.) The point is that when you combine what's happening in the smart appliance world, the explosion of smart phones and tablets, and social media, what you're getting is a white-hot combination for marketers who want to create more and more targeted advertisements for potential consumers. This all takes computing power and the ability to harvest data from many different data sources. The surge in "Big Data" is making clouds more and more economical to deal with surges, without having to overbuild.

This change is also making it easier and easier for new business units or new businesses to stand up very complex customer services. Here's a question that more and more enterprise IT executives are asking: Why can't you just buy a Customer Relations Management (CRM) system such as Salesforce.com or Microsoft Dynamics®, or an Enterprise Resource Planning (ERP) system off the shelf? All the major players in the virtualization world are pushing systems that allow you to deploy complete systems as a single piece instead of having to shop for the pieces separately. In this respect, we would say that WordPress® is a harbinger of "cloudy" things to come.

WordPress is a framework in which developers are creating massive numbers of templates so that businesses can grab a Web presence off the shelf and then pay for smaller (and less expensive) customizations to make the sites truly theirs. The developers are taking a risk that business will like how their templates look and that they'll be able to make a profit by writing to the framework that is WordPress. What we're waiting for in the cloud business model is more standardization so that economy of scale will draw more developers into the market. We can certainly imagine that something like OpenStack® might be the platform of scale that will drive the cloud marketplace just as the AppStore has driven the iPhone®/iPad® revolution.

Platform or Sandbox

Software developers have always wanted a "draft site" so that they could test their systems in a live environment, but getting management to approve a duplicate system was, for many organizations, a fantasy. The return on investment (ROI) for a draft system just wasn't possible to justify until virtualization came along. However, now that draft systems can be cloned off production systems in minutes, developers can build and deploy a draft quickly and inexpensively. Even better, it's now affordable to not only stand up a draft system but also stand up virtual workstations that can generate synthetic traffic. The ease of cloning entire systems has made "sandboxing" not only possible but also economical through more extensive testing to avoid costly downtime or incompatibilities. Customized systems can now be launched in a sandbox and tested against a clone of the production system at the software house, thus obviating the need to be on site. New systems made possible by these developments include private virtual switches (vSwitches) that isolate virtual server traffic from the outside world as well as database and middleware servers that could potentially have their own virtual auditing system(s). The industry is now taking this concept a step further with the concept of containerization. Once a system has been created, you can now use a containerization system such as Docker (http://www.docker.com) to gather up the entire system into a single "container" to make deployment of complex systems dramatically easier. Interestingly enough, containers are also inherently read-only, which has a side benefit of making rollbacks of malware infected systems easier.

Another great example of sandboxing has emerged in the form of workstation virtualization. Now that workstation horsepower is generally up to the task, you can launch and run entire systems on a desktop or laptop computer. System prototyping on workstations can now include virtual appliances such as firewalls, remote-access gateways, load balancers, virtual networks, and just about anything you'd be likely to have on your physical network.

A frequently overlooked benefit is that you can quickly clone an entire existing system in order to test out upgrades. Engineers can test system or application upgrades on a clone system, which doesn't have any impact on IT production if it must be discarded due to a failed upgrade. The logical conclusion of sandboxing is obvious but can be taken one step further. Most of the major players are allowing you to package these sandboxes as a single entity. Instead of forcing you to deploy the individual pieces according to some complex procedure, this packaging gives the developer(s) a chance to set up private vswitches and collections of virtual machines and resources into packages that be deployed in a single straightforward process. In addition, with the introduction of "self-service IT," this concept can now be extended through resource pools that authorized users draw upon to self-provision systems—for example, a department that has xxx TB of storage, yy virtual CPUs, nnn vswitches, and so forth, which can be drawn upon by authorized users.

Although this is very clearly a conversation about "Platform as a Service," the point being made here is that the IT world has changed a model that required developers to pick from a long menu of items to one that allows administrators to roll out collections of resources *and* applications from a single catalog entry. The bigger point is that there is now less chance of someone forgetting to deploy an important operational component (e.g., the organization's syslog server or Simple Network Management Protocol (SNMP) management connections) since it's now an appliance. What's even better here is that you can thin provision even complex systems since you don't necessarily need to create a complete copy "from scratch" but can start the system off the organizational master image and only create newly provisioned storage for the changes you make to the new copy. You can compare the process to booting all the CRM systems from a single read-only copy and, once the system is started, swapping to a much smaller storage allocation to simply hold customizations unique to the instance. This also provides a great way to update all the CRM instances with a single update (or break all the CRMs in one fell swoop, if you fail to test first).

The lesson? Clone your production instance of software and systems and tinker away in relative safety.

Platform as a Service (PaaS) Issues:

Pros

- Buy-in cost is low; just rent what you need.
- Maintenance is typically embedded in your rental costs.
- Hardware failure typically means the providers just shift your virtual environment to a different set of systems.
- Entire collections of virtual machines can be deployed as a single system.
- Building "draft" machines or systems is now fairly easy.

Cons

- You can't walk down the hall to work on a machine; physical access means creating a trouble ticket.
- You're on a shared platform (mostly).
- Performance could potentially swing wildly, depending upon the terms of your service-level agreement (SLA).
- Now all access is remote access.
- Spinning up a draft may be easy, but you still have to pay for the incremental costs for the new virtual machine.

To summarize, Platform as a Service (PaaS) is really about buying the resources to stand up full servers, virtual networks, and other v-pieces. You still have to worry about patches, updates, and loading applications, just as you did in your own data center.

Chapter 9

Software as a Service

In many ways, cloud computing got its start with Software as a Service (SaaS). Applications provided from a remote service on a subscription model provided the "proof of concept" that many IT executives needed to see before they would commit to moving away from the traditional on-premise application and service hosting that had been the norm for decades.

SaaS is distinguished from the other ". . . as a Service" clouds by providing complete applications—rather than services, functions, or infrastructure components—to the organization and its users.

As we've already discussed, a variety of economic and technology factors have led to growth in SaaS to the point that, in many industries and application types, SaaS is now the "normal" way of delivering application services, whereas on-premises deployments are reserved for unusual cases. Despite this, security is still seen as an issue for many organizations that are otherwise ready for a jump to the cloud.

SaaS becomes part of the security discussion in three different scenarios:

- SaaS applications that must be secured
- Data flowing to and from SaaS applications that must be secured
- SaaS applications that provide security to other applications and data

Let's take a look at each of these and see how the SaaS architecture plays a role in what is possible—and how it can happen.

The Internet Defines SaaS

Two SaaS Delivery Models

SaaS is available, considered broadly, in two configurations: hosted application management and software on demand. In the first model, you can think of a service provider pulling virtual copies of software off the shelf and handing them out to customers, each customer receiving an individual copy of the software. In the second model, all the customers share access to a single copy of the software, with user authentication and individual storage responsible for keeping data separate and secure.

All Users Work from a Single Software Version

One of the primary sources of vulnerability is the lack of fully patched and updated software in the application delivery chain. It becomes especially critical and problematic when some systems within the computer fleet have been patched and others have not—especially if the IT operations team believes that the fleet is fully patched.

In SaaS operation models featuring a single operating system and application image that is used for each new user instance, many of the complications around patching and updating disappear. In this model, a single copy of software has to be updated; after that, it is certain that every user will be operating from a fully up-to-date version of the application.

Easy to Upgrade, Manage, and Deploy Software

There's no mystery to one of the major factors in the benefits of the SaaS model to IT operations groups: It's far easier to update one system than to update hundreds. Not only that, it's far easier to know which version of software is being used at any given time when every instance is running from the same master.

The difficulty and expense of patching hundreds or thousands of individual systems is one of the reasons frequently given for applications and operating systems remaining un-patched in the enterprise. A SaaS model eliminates much of the complication inherent in update management, though it does leave one significant issue still to be worked out.

In many cases, software developers take advantage of operating system functions that turn out to be unique to specific versions of the OS. In traditional on-premises software deployment, the user organization or its software vendor is responsible for making sure that application software is compatible with new versions of the operating system.

Frequently, enterprise application incompatibility is listed as a reason for not performing operating system upgrades. An advantage of the SaaS model is that the SaaS provider is responsible for developing applications with limited OS version dependencies and ensuring that all dependencies are dealt with prior to deploying the software to any customers.

That responsibility is the cornerstone of the shared responsibility (or security) model that is the operative model at most cloud service providers today.

Shared Responsibility Model

Amazon Web Services™ (AWS™) is, at the time of this writing, the largest Infrastructure as a Service (IaaS) provider in the world. As such, many terms and definitions put forward by AWS are adopted by other providers of various sorts. One of the terms, not necessarily developed by AWS but certainly used by the company, is the "shared responsibility model" of security (https://aws.amazon.com/compliance/shared-responsibility-model/).

Simply stated, the shared responsibility model is as follows:

- The cloud provider is responsible for the security of the set of services it provides—the hardware certainly, and possibly the operating system, functions, and applications as defined by the service agreement.
- The cloud customer is responsible for the security of the data that flows into, off of, and through the hardware, software, and services purchased from the cloud provider.

The practical effect of the shared responsibility model is therefore that the cloud provider is responsible for keeping the systems up, running, and secure from intruders. If something should happen and hackers actually get into the system, though, it's your responsibility to make sure that anything they get their hands on isn't useful.

Since its introduction by Amazon, the shared security model has been embraced by many of the large public cloud providers, including Microsoft® Azure® (https://blogs.msdn.microsoft.com/azure security/2016/04/18/what-does-shared-responsibility-in-the-cloud-mean/), CenturyLink® (https://www.ctl.io/compliance/cloud-security-shared-responsibility/), and Google® (https://cloud.google.com/security/). There are small differences in the way that the different services interpret precise demarcation lines between customer and provider responsibility, but the principle remains the same in all examples.

Security appliance and service vendors have recognized the opportunity inherent in the shared security model and released a wide variety of products and services that function to protect data while respecting (or, in some cases, working in conjunction with) cloud security capabilities deployed by providers to protect the infrastructure.

Cloud-specific security products will take advantage of open application programming interfaces (APIs) to bring a unified security stance to the divided responsibilities of the shared security model. This single solution to a multi-responsibility problem is especially critical for those working within a rigorous regulatory environment such as the Health Insurance Portability and Accountability Act of 1996 (HIPAA). Within these environments, the responsible organization must prove compliance regardless of which company is actually providing the security. A single application coordinating and managing security throughout the application infrastructure can be a vital ingredient in protecting both information safety and IT staff sanity.

There are, of course, many ways in which a customer can provide security for the data they own, but effective protection depends on functions and practices bundled into two product categories: Cloud Access Security Brokers (CASB) and Cloud Access Gateways (CAGs).

Cloud Access Security Brokers

One of the first companies to introduce a product labeled as "Cloud Access Security Broker," or CASB, Skyhigh Networks defined four functions as the pillars of CASB—Visibility, Compliance, Data Security, and

Threat Protection. Each of the four can be provided in separate services or appliances, but many organizations have decided that ease of deployment and management are best provided by a security solution that brings all four together in a single logical entity. Many of the concepts in the following four sections originated in Skyhigh Networks' original definitions of the terms within CASB (https://www.skyhighnetworks.com/cloud-security-university/what-is-cloud-access-security-broker/).

Visibility

Initially, CASB offerings sought to do one thing—tell cloud computing customers precisely which services and applications made up their application environment. This is a far more complex question than it might initially seem for two important reasons: First, although a cloud customer presumably knows which cloud applications they are directly contracting with (more on this later), they may not know all the cloud services that make up those primary applications. Those "sub-contractors" are part of the cloud infrastructure even if their contract is with one of the other cloud services and not the end customer.

Next, there are still companies that live under the presumption that their IT department is responsible for every cloud service and application in use within the company's network borders. This is not the case in so many instances that a term was coined to describe it: "Shadow IT."

Shadow IT takes two forms: The first is business units and managers who buy cloud applications and services with purchase orders that fall within their financial limits or even through credit card charges that are paid through expense account reporting. Some of these services and applications don't interface with other applications used within the organization and simply involve business time and (perhaps) sensitive data. Others interact with existing databases and applications through APIs that the rogue cloud service can use to silently hook into the corporate infrastructure.

The second form of shadow IT is made up of consumer-grade cloud applications and services that individual employees use during the course of their day. These can range from social media services used for collaboration, to cloud data storage tools such as Dropbox® or Google Drive™, and personal productivity tools including calendar, word processing, and presentation applications.

In any case, the organization cannot protect data and processes if it doesn't know the applications and services in use. CASB begins with a rigorous survey of the business infrastructure to draw up a list of all the applications, apps, tools, and services in use—and to determine which data resources those applications and services are interacting with.

Compliance

In many cases, regulatory compliance has been the primary driver of data security spending and deployment for decades. There have been conflicting opinions about whether this is a good thing. Some argue that many companies would completely ignore security if regulatory penalties did not force their hand, whereas others bemoan the fact that regulatory requirements frequently become the final statement on security rather than the minimum starting position.

Once the cloud application environment is fully and accurately mapped, decisions can be made on how to bring data processing, handling, and storage into compliance with pertinent regulations. Perhaps as important, CASB services offer verification of compliance—verification that can be presented to compliance auditors when audit time arrives.

When compliance considerations arise, they are specific to the industry regulations or legal jurisdiction pertaining to the individual organization. In the United States, regulations and standards such as HIPAA, the Family Educational Rights and Privacy Act (FERPA), and the Payment Card Industry Data Security Standard (PCI DSS) impose strict requirements and harsh penalties for their violation.

In Canada, the Personal Information Protection and Electronic Documents Act (PIPEDA) is the regulatory framework guiding most organizations in their commercial or federal activities.

The most recent data privacy laws are those within the EU's General Data Privacy Regulation (GDPR) system, which took effect in early 2018. GDPR is intended to apply the same data privacy laws across the EU and to extend those protections to all EU citizens. It's that last part which has many organizations around the world paying attention to GDPR, since a single customer or student with EU citizenship means that an organization's IT operations fall under GDPR regulation.

Data Security

Threat Protection

Beyond discovery and coordination, CASB systems also provide active protection for data and infrastructure. CASB can utilize proxy technology (both forward and reverse) and a huge library of APIs to work with applications and services across on-premises and cloud environments.

Depending on the specific CASB, the product may protect data at rest and in motion by enforcing rules, applying filters, creating VPNs, authenticating identities and services, and doing a variety of other things within the application infrastructure. Conversely, the CASB may provide all of these benefits by controlling and managing other products and services as they directly provide the protection.

One of the attractions of the CASB model is the flexibility it offers. Once the system goes through the discovery phase, it can protect what it discovers in many different ways, going so far as to protect different cloud components using different methods all under unified control.

CASB Spreads Security Across SaaS and On-Prem

Among the differences in methods is a split between those who deploy CASB as SaaS and those who prefer to have it as an on-premises solution. While the capabilities are rapidly evolving, one of the factors driving this decision is how the CASB will interact with critical pieces of the application infrastructure—whether, that is, through API or proxy.

There's little question that API deployment can allow, at least in theory, somewhat greater depth of integration between CASB and infrastructure because the protection can then be applied within the application, rather than across boundaries. (For more on this, see the section on microsegmentation later in this chapter.)

On the other hand, proxy-based CASB deployments are, at the time of this writing, becoming the more popular of the two options for two major reasons: deployment ease and scalability. Proxies are easier to deploy because their use often requires no additional programming within the application. At most, URLs and request response expectations may need to change.

In addition, deploying a CASB as a proxy implemented by SaaS means that the CASB vendor is responsible for adequate performance as the traffic load scales to the limits of the contracted levels. Scalability combined with the flexibility that comes with a cloud implementation makes the proxy/SaaS combination the one that is, in early 2018, the most popular deployment choice.

Use Cases for SaaS

Even with great popularity, there's no guarantee that a particular deployment model will work for every situation. Deciding on the proper use case for SaaS, CASB is a process similar to that of deciding on the proper use case for SaaS deployment of other applications. All security is a balancing act between cost and safety. All cloud computing deployments are balancing acts between control and capability. Finding the balances along the various axes is critical for successful SaaS deployment of CASB (or, for that matter, any security application.)

Containers Are Developer-Driven SaaS Tools

When SaaS is taken to a logical technical conclusion, you end up with a deployment in which an entire application delivery platform, including all dependent applications and services, is packaged and delivered as a unit. That unit, today, is called a container, and containers have become a major driving force in the continuing evolution of virtualized and abstracted platforms.

The most important thing to realize about containers is that they are complete images of an application with its environment. This makes containers very popular with developers because they don't have to worry about versions or service dependencies that might not be present in the development environment: With containers, everything is there in every instance!

That completeness is also the containers' greatest weakness because a vulnerability or piece of malware that is present in the "master" copy of the environment will be present in every copy and every instance. This means that there are two critical steps to securing container applications. The first is thorough, careful screening of every application and service in the master image for vulnerabilities and malware. Problems that are solved in the master don't make it into the copies.

The second step is, in essence, to not trust the first. Just because you (or another person or group) has tested and screened the master doesn't mean that security screening can be skipped in further instances. Continued vigilance is required because new vulnerabilities are being found in operating systems and applications.

Both steps are best implemented in ways that minimize the requirement for a human to become involved. Since containers are frequently deployed in a devops environment, security processes should be automated along with all the other deployment processes involved in implementing the containers. Doing this effectively means involving security during the planning and development stages—something that is a cultural problem in many organizations.

It's easy to get wrapped up in the technological and process-oriented parts of security: In many cases, including containers, the cultural and human-relations parts of security can be just as important.

Microsegmentation

Every time there is a boundary or interface between two (or more) components of an application, there is an attack surface—an opportunity for attack and intrusion. In the "classic" security model, a hardened perimeter would be built around the entire application so that data could flow between internal components with no security concerns. As we have discussed throughout this book, it's no longer sufficient to assume that the perimeter will hold. Every transition and connection must be suspect.

When no connection or application component is trusted, the model is called "microsegmentation." It is also quite accurately referred to as the "zero trust model." In this model, a security perimeter is drawn around every component, and authentication is required at every step. In many instances, data is encrypted and decrypted at every transition, as well.

Some claim that microsegmentation creates excessive overhead for the application environment and that the cost in complications and performance penalties is too high. Proponents of the method point out that modern systems are rarely performance-limited by hardware and that the improvements in security are worth whatever penalty must be paid in performance.

Microsegmentation's rise has echoed that of network virtualization and software-defined networking (SDN). When network segments are being redefined and redeployed on a rapid, automated basis, it makes sense to re-authenticate and re-verify at every instance.

Whether in traditional SaaS, containers, or whatever architecture will succeed them, the issue of trust is paramount in security. In a highly dynamic and constantly varying environment, zero trust has become the logical conclusion of a policy of maximum paranoia. It is a conclusion that makes sense when the goal is to automate applications but not the vulnerabilities and attacks that prey upon them.

Chapter 10

Virtual Desktop Infrastructure

Virtual Desktop Infrastructure or VDI (http://en.wikipedia.org/wiki/Desktop_virtualization#Virtual_desktop_infrastructure) is often unfairly compared to its predecessor Microsoft® Terminal Server (http://technet.microsoft.com/en-us/library/cc755399(v=WS.10).aspx). Although they look similar to each other at the user level, they are most definitely very different technologies. Let's define the two and explore the ways in which VDI is similar to, although a more natural extension of, the base Terminal Services technology.

Terminal Services: This technology has its roots in the multiuser kernel originally developed as part of the Windows NT® Server 4.0. It has been enhanced and extended over the years to become part of Windows Server®, regardless of whether Terminal Services has been enabled or not, as can be seen in Figure 10.1. It should also be noted that in Windows NT® 3.51, Citrix® licensed the source code from Microsoft and created WinFrame®, which implemented a multiuser version of Windows®.

Terminal Services has some obvious roots in the more traditional timesharing found in the Unix® world. If you recall that Windows NT®'s father was David Cutler, who was also instrumental in the creation of the operating systems used by Digital Equipment Corporation's VAX (http://

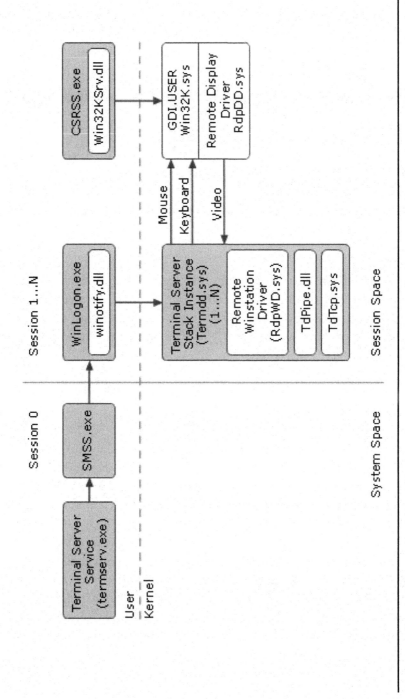

Figure 10.1. Terminal services architecture.

en.wikipedia.org/wiki/Dave_Cutler), it's no wonder that the base archi-tecture looks so familiar to industry old-timers. As with Unix, you can have a limited level of user customization (including desktops, apps, look, and feel), but the system still creates multiuser desktops/sessions based upon the base server operating system.

The most obvious limitation of the system is that Terminal Services is slicing the base server system's resources into multiple desktop sessions (known as Multiuser Windows). The Microsoft Terminal Service imple-mentation also has the ability to set up a gateway to direct the remote connection to a slave desktop workstation. Originally called Terminal Services Connection Broker, the Remote Desktop Connection Broker got a new name and a significant set of enhancements as part of a bridge tech-nology that saw a move from slaved desktops and time-sliced terminal sessions origins to a true virtual desktop system by leveraging the hypervi-sor virtualization technologies that first emerged as Microsoft Virtual PC (which ran as an application on top of a Windows operating system). This eventually became the Microsoft hypervisor that became an integral part of Windows Server® 2008 (http://en.wikipedia.org/wiki/Hyper-V).

A notable progression was the addition of several new features when Terminal Services changed its name to Remote Desktop Protocol (RDP). Two notable improvements to the RDP suite was the addition of a gate-way feature that enabled multiple users to funnel through a single network connection secured by an active directory authentication. This gateway broker also provided methodologies to implement group policies at login so that the incoming connection could be directed to a person's desk-top computer. A second notable improvement was Remote Applications Integrated Locally [(R.A.I.L.); http://msdn.microsoft.com/en-us/library/Cc239612.aspx] where only a single application interface is presented in the RDP window instead of a whole desktop. In the Citrix world, this feature is called XenApp® and has been part of the Citrix product line for a very long time.

Virtual Desktop Infrastructure: This is a marriage of many of the com-ponents from the original Microsoft Terminal Services but differs because it utilizes a Type I hypervisor (in which the hypervisor runs on the base hardware rather than on a host operating system) to host fully virtualized machines instead of time slicing a single instance or redirecting opera-tions to a dedicated physical workstation through the gateway connec-tion broker, as shown in Figure 10.2. This dramatically more efficient

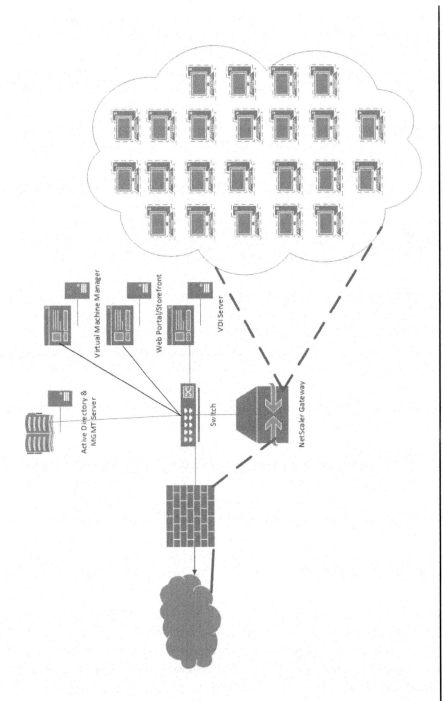

Figure 10.2. Gateway connection broker illustration.

technology is commonly acknowledged as the primary reason why there has been a recent resurgence in thin client interest.

The flexibility of now being able to remotely connect to foreign operating systems (i.e., Linux®, Windows® XP, Windows® 7, etc.) not only provides a greater level of flexibility but also allows for a degree of hardware abstraction giving new life to legacy operating systems and applications. All the major players in this market have the ability to support multiple flavors of virtual hardware (network interface cards, disk emulation, etc.) that provide for both legacy and modern interfaces. This way, a legacy app that can perhaps only run under the older 32-bit Windows XP can still be supported in a virtual environment. In just about every case, tools exist to migrate physical machines to the virtual environment using either supplied (P2V) or third-party tools. In the case of the migration system from companies such as Paragon Software, the migration tools very closely resemble a system-level backup but instead create a virtual hard drive that can then be imported into VMware® or Microsoft® Hyper-V®.

It should certainly be noted that Microsoft's remote computing strategy is closely tied to the ability to share one's desktop session information over an RDP, which, over the years, has increased functionality and security capabilities as Microsoft has released new versions of their desktop operating system (http://en.wikipedia.org/wiki/Remote_Desktop_Protocol). The constellation of tools in the remote access world is now being labeled VDI, which has evolved to connote complete heterogeneous virtualized workstations, authentication, encryption, and management.

The Microsoft VDI solution is more than just a single protocol; it is rather a constellation of closely linked services that can be set up in a nearly infinite number of combinations. Here, it might be good to compare the two most popular technologies and terminologies used to describe the VDI constellation of systems:

Virtual Application Windows, called App-V by Microsoft and XenApp® by Citrix.
Virtual Machine Desktops, called VDI by Microsoft and XenDesktop® by Citrix.

This is a good place to acknowledge that Citrix's Metaframe version of Windows NT was the first to take advantage of the multiuser capabilities that were architected but unfilled in the first version of the operating system. Although we're sure the marketing groups of the players would all love to say they invented this genre, we feel fairly safe in saying that a great amount of cross-pollination has taken place over the last couple of decades, with all parties benefitting.

Virtual Desktops—The Cloud from the Other End

Whether you call it XenDesktop or VDI, XenApp or App-V, the difference is that you're creating an infrastructure to connect to a heterogeneous collection of foreign operating systems provisioned either on a collection of physical desktop machines or a collection of virtual machines, typically on a type I hypervisor.

Jokingly called "sticking your head in the clouds," the VDI concept simply entails putting a workstation operating system into a virtualized environment and providing some sort of way to connect to it in what is hopefully a secure manner. The differences are in how each of the cloud vendors have added their own custom features and functions to those connections. How those connections are implemented and managed has been and will be the true differentiators, as Microsoft pushes RDP and (more recently) RemoteFX®, Citrix pushes HDX, and VMware pushes PC over IP (PCOIP) remote access variations.

Another differentiator is in how each solution handles graphics and where the heavy lifting of the 3D imagery is done. Conceptually, what most vendors have done is remove the necessity to send large amounts of 3D imagery over the network connection and instead provide capabilities for using for hardware graphic processors in the server. This allows the 3D models to travel shorter, faster paths internal to the server instead of forcing them to move over the (much slower) network. What both vendors have implemented is 3D rendering at the server, thereby only sending much smaller 2D snapshots over the network to the workstation.

In the case of Citrix, you need to be running a CUDA core–based graphics processing unit (GPU) in a XenServer®-based hypervisor; and in the case of Microsoft, you need to be running on at least a Windows Server® 2008 R2 SP1–based Hyper-V machine. Citrix describes this arrangement as "GPU Passthru," whereas Microsoft is sharing the GPU as a system resource. The obvious markets for this sort of advanced graphics processing include scientific computing (i.e., MATLAB®, AutoCAD®, ArcGIS®, etc.) as well as providing thin clients or remote clients a user experience similar to those on full-sized workstations locally connected to servers using the newer Aero 3D interfaces, HD video playback, and USB redirection for peripherals.

Some of the limitations of server-based GPUs result from how that hardware resource is shared. At the time of writing, the Citrix system can be described as a one-to-one (1:1) arrangement wherein, for each time slice, the GPU Passthru users get 100% of the GPU resources, whereas in the Microsoft RemoteFX world, the number of users that can share that resource is based upon the resolution requested and the number of monitors requested. The scenario is based upon the amount of video RAM available in the GPU, which translates to more monitors and the higher resolution per monitor possible per RemoteFX workstation (http://technet.microsoft.com/en-us/library/ff830364.aspx). The analogy we like is that RemoteFX plays Tetris® with the virtual desktop graphical resource requests to maximize the number of users that can be serviced in each time slice—that is, a virtual workstation asking for dual 1080p-resolution monitors with 24bits of color depth will use up most of the GPU RAM available on the server, so RemoteFX can only shoe horn in a single monitor 16bit color depth virtual workstation session in this first time slice. However, in the next time slice, RemoteFX can now service 32 single monitor sessions, since the monster dual monitor virtual session doesn't need to be refreshed in this time slice. Perhaps an even better analogy is a car ferry that can carry 32 regular cars, but only a single tour bus and a few cars per river crossing.

Much Lower Deployment, Maintenance, and Management Costs

VDI is one of those concepts that have a tendency to be mis-sold in terms of expectations. Management keeps hearing only that thin clients cost a fraction of what full desktops cost and that they don't need as many in-person technical support visits. What they don't hear is that the backend infrastructure must change in order to successfully deploy a VDI system. The key here is that you could very well *not* save money in the short term but instead reap savings in the long run. VDI is one of those technologies that shift costs and complexity from the user desktop to the backend server farm. Let's look at the most basic components to watch the shift.

Money at the desktop workstation:

1. You need applications and operating system licenses.
2. You need help desk support for your users.
3. You need a network connection at the desktop.
4. You need peripherals such as monitors, keyboards, headsets, web-cams, etc.
5. Those full-sized workstations have dropped in price to under $1K, but thin clients can be as low as $50 (Dell™/Wyse™).
6. Analyst firms such as Gartner are reporting Total Cost of Ownership (TCO) costs in excess of five times the original purchase price due to support issues (http://www.gartner.com/newsroom/id/636308). It's just more expensive to have technical support physically visit a desktop PC.
7. Failed or cancelled updates could potentially provide significant infection vectors for malware.
8. Proprietary or confidential information goes out the door anytime a desktop PC is removed for repair/upgrade/etc. Even cache and swap information can be very revealing.

Money for VDI:

1. You still need applications and operating system licenses.
2. You still need help desk support for your users.
3. You still need a network connection at the desktop.
4. You still need peripherals such as monitors, keyboards, headsets, webcams, etc.
5. If you use a thin/zero client, you can now send out a new machine in interoffice mail.
6. A zero client doesn't store any confidential or proprietary information; it's just like the old "green screen" terminals.
7. You no longer need to succumb to paranoid user requests for a UPS at the desktop.
8. The VDI server is MUCH more expensive than a desktop PC but may be less expensive than upgrading all your desktop PCs.
9. The VDI server can't use an inexpensive GPU, and at the time of writing, the number of GPUs officially supported is quite small. ATI/AMD does have a line of server-based GPUs that are officially supported for server duty (http://www.amd.com/us/products/work

station/graphics/software/Pages/remote-graphics-vdi.aspx)—one product line for Remote graphics (GPU pass thru) for VMware and Citrix, and another for shared GPUs (RemoteFX) for Microsoft.

10. New to Microsoft Server® 2012 R2 is full support for software GPU functions that get you away from special-purpose VDI GPUs by trading off CPU cycles.

11. Each user still needs storage for personal configurations, user-specific software, wallpaper, etc. All the major players also support template-based user sessions in which everyone runs the same base virtual machine and all user changes to the desktop are thrown away after log off.

12. Not everything or everyone is appropriate for VDI. At the time of writing video conferencing and some scientific applications fall into the "not appropriate" category. The echo cancellation algorithms used in VDI tend to break when the codec software is too far separated from the physical device, either through latency or jitter. Another example of a problematic VDI application involves massive simulations that require dedicated access to ultra-large graphics processing power. These will almost always provide performance that disappoints users if VDI is used for the deployment. It has only been recently that remote-access vendors—for example, Citrix—have integrated technology such as audio codecs (code/decode software) into the endpoint systems in order to fix audio synchronization problems with applications like Skype®.

Like servers, VDI can dramatically benefit from the sandbox effect discussed in Chapter 8 since it's now trivial to create a new workstation image. Anytime the IT group would have to reinstall the operating system on a new machine is now an opportunity to save time by using sandbox images. All the major private and public cloud players have the ability to store templates in some sort of library facility that, in some cases, can become a self-service portal for users to build their own systems. For academic institutions, it's now possible to have an instructor create one "perfect" system and then use that as a template. It has become more and more common for one class to run a legacy application in Windows XP while the following class could log in and see Linux workstations all governed by the students logging into a portal that directs them to the virtual workstation image for that class.

Another huge part of the total cost of ownership is maintenance and the responsibility of making sure that each workstation is updated. The Achilles' heel of remote workstation maintenance systems is the user. Those machines need to be turned on to be updated, and although "Wake on LAN" (http://en.wikipedia.org/wiki/Wake_on_lan) seems to work, it won't work if the users are energy conscious and turn their entire desks off at the power strip.

What VDI now gives you is the ability to update both the operating system and applications even if the virtual desktop is powered down. Systems such as Microsoft's System Center Virtual Machine Manager® even allow you to schedule waves of updates to those virtual desktops to avoid overloading the host server. Similar facilities are either available or will soon be available from all the major VDI players.

This type of flexibility also opens up the possibility of archiving these virtual machines into some sort of library or exporting them to some sort of removable media. Just the ability to "park" a virtual machine greatly extends the ability to accommodate environments traditionally too expensive to consider in the past—that is, the professor doesn't need it over the summer break, so why let them take up system resources?

The bottom line is that you need to look at the total system cost—not just the desktop. VDI is *not* a magic bullet against high cost but rather a way to provide similar or enhanced services at a lower cost of ownership long term, through support and management costs.

One Desktop Experience: Many Client Platforms

Although much of the industry is entranced by the TCO issue with VDI, the remote desktop access on heterogeneous remote platforms is what really made Citrix famous. With over a decade head start on its competition, Citrix has made a huge name for itself by making its Redirector product available on just about every modern computing platform (and some that aren't modern, or even still in the market). For a very long time, Citrix was a lone voice in the remote access world (well, except for the *nix community*).

---

* *nix is an industry abbreviation for all the Unix® variations (Linux® and Unix are both *nix aka wildcard+nix. [*Source:* https://en.wikipedia.org/wiki/Unix-like]).

What VDI is offering is not unlike what we used to have on mainframes of old: mainframe-like central management and provisioning with terminal-like desktops, but with the flexibility of the modern desktop operating system. The icing on the cake is that since all the heavy lifting is being done on the server, the human interface load on the network is reduced to the point at which the remote connection can be run on almost any platform. If you want to get an architect to start drooling, just show them AutoDesk® Revit® or AutoCAD® 3D running on an iPad®. The first time you spin that 3D model by sweeping your fingers you'll have them hooked. Let's face it. The general users don't want to have to learn the details of caring for and feeding their desktop PCs; they just want them to work. They also want massive computing capabilities everywhere they go, and they want it even over marginal mobile connections.

Let's look a bit at what's happening behind the scenes to fulfill that wish. First and foremost, *nothing* is free. Even with shifting the 3D heavy lifting from the desktop to the virtual host, you still need to send compressed 2D images to the remote client *very* quickly for applications such as video. You highly compress the images to reduce the overall bandwidth necessary, but then those compressed images have to be uncompressed at the client end. Something to keep in mind about thin clients in general is that they're running a CPU that is not very different from that in a mobile phone, and uncompressing any audio or video file is either going to be done by the CPU or by some type of dedicated hardware (i.e., some of Texas Instruments' Digital Signal Processing chips). This, more than anything else, determines just how well the thin client handles video playback and the maximum possible display resolution.

CPUs, GPUs, and compression algorithms aren't all that system architects must take into account when it comes to thin clients. Another thing to investigate is the connection protocol and the codecs that those remote clients use. In the beginning, there was Terminal Server, and although it worked, it had some limitations—enough limitations that vendors sought to create variations to expand the Terminal Server to work better in various specialized situations. Then came the Remote Desktop Protocol, which improved security, speed, and the ability to work over wide area networks (http://en.wikipedia.org/wiki/Remote_Desktop_Protocol). The result, and the challenging part of this dance, is that the connection technology in the Microsoft world is closely tied to the version of your server's operating system, with Microsoft's newest RemoteFX only being supported on server operating system versions since Windows Server 2008 R2 SP1.

Unfortunately, there is not much information available for the consumer to differentiate RDP versions that contain the RemoteFX enhancement. You're expected to know that RemoteFX is only available in RDP versions on Windows 7 and newer operating systems. You can, however, turn on backwards compatibility (see Figure 10.3) even in Windows

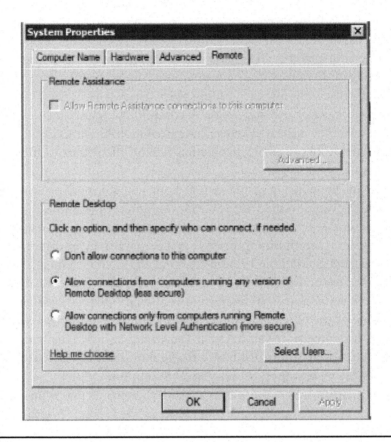

Figure 10.3. The control panel object in Windows Server® 2008 to configure backwards compatibility for RDP connections.

Server 2008, but turning this on means that even older and less-secure versions of Remote Desktop can connect to your server. The most secure native option for Windows remote access is called Network Level Authentication (NLA) and is represented as the bottommost option in Figure 10.3, with the middle option being secure—but nowhere near as secure as NLA. It should be noted that Wikipedia®'s article on RDP has a superb table showing versions of RDP and compatibility (http://en.wikipedia.org/wiki/Remote_Desktop_Protocol).

This compatibility dance has occurred in the Citrix world as well, but has been largely hidden from view through automatic updates to the Reflector client and server. Our guess is that this perception advantage is why Citrix continues support for such a huge variety of clients. With the ability to control both client- and server-side communications protocols, this "hiding in plain view" has been nearly invisible to users. The point here is that Citrix and Microsoft have been in a love/hate relationship over remote access—both partner and competitor. Citrix has taken advantage of Microsoft's complex set-up requirements for nearly the same functions and made the process both simpler and non–vendor specific with support for VMware, Microsoft, and their own XenServer. Another advantage for Citrix is that the XenApp and XenDesktop systems can be configured to fit on the VMware, Microsoft, and Citrix hypervisor hosts. At the date of writing, Microsoft has remained Windows-centric for remote access clients, with only two vendors supporting RemoteFX on Apple® OS X® and IOS®.

Performance in Question for VDI

What this compatibility dance really has done is create a confusing kaleidoscope of remote access solutions with just as many performance caveats. The first problem is that performance in the remote access game isn't just about numbers; it's also about user experience. The reality is that if users are comfortable with a system boot process that takes xxx seconds to get to the login user prompt, VDI needs to get to the same point in roughly the same amount of time. Users get used to the flash of the user interface. Just look at how popular the fish tank screen saver became during the Windows XP time frame.

An example of not taking this human factor into account was certainly a contributing factor in terminal services gaining a less-than-favorable reputation when some implementers failed to take into account user resistance to extended login times. This is a situation where we're strong believers in testing that includes user experience testing, even if it's only in a sandbox. This test must include asking critical questions and taking important steps such as checking to see if your testing procedure accounts for load scaling. Is the performance of six test users on a scaled-down VDI server the same as a hundred on a production server? Perhaps part of your testing should be on an intermediate-sized system to see the impact of CPU power and memory on virtual client performance. No matter what the salesperson says, we've *never* found a typical user desktop, and only internal testing can accurately reflect your organization.

Other huge factors to consider are network bottlenecks, which create variable amounts of delays, depending upon overall network traffic. Some of the original remote desktop solutions were based upon TCP connections that would automatically back off during congestion situations, thereby forcing large numbers of retransmissions and further increasing congestions and delay. Newer systems designed for better WAN connectivity have been implemented by both Microsoft and Citrix and are now based on UDP for a network transport with advanced error correction, so that loss and out-of-order packets are either ignored or reconstructed mathematically. We have seen too many organizations simply believe the sales pitch that a VDI solution "will just work," without confirming the facts for themselves. Take advantage of how all the major VDI players have free reviewer licenses to take the system for a test drive; at the very least, your IT group can get their hands dirty so they can better predict the human costs for support. One *huge* issue with remote access (VDI,

Figure 10.4. The InterWorking Labs® "Mini Maxwell™" portable network emulator. (*Source*: https://iwl.com/products/kmax. Reproduced with permission from © 1995–2018 InterWorking Labs, Inc. dba IWL.)

terminal services, Web, etc.) is confirming just how well your applications utilize the bandwidth.

Some friends of ours at InterWorking Labs, Inc. created a product called a Mini Maxwell™ (http://iwl.com/products/kmax), shown in Figure 10.4, which purposely degrades a standard Ethernet interface to simulate anything from the errors and latency you would expect from a cross-country link to the nasty surprises one might find on a satellite link. Their demonstration video uses cruise ship Internet connections as an illustration of how the simulated link could help your application developers reduce sensitivity to high-latency connections.

The Security/Alteration "Lock Down" from Central Management

The advantage of a full operating system at the desktop is also the greatest weakness. With greater flexibility comes greater potential for configuration and greater possibility for someone to find a weakness to exploit. The industry has come up with an amazing array of potential solutions to lock down those workstations and turn them into a "trusted platform." We're seeing group policies, TPM chips, change rollback systems, and some truly convoluted systems—all designed to secure desktop operating systems.

The key thing to remember is that if you have a general-purpose operating system on the desktop, you also have a computing platform that could potentially be exploited against you. To this end, security professionals have gone to great lengths to ensure that these machines are secured against unauthorized changes, and that any type of sensitive changes is audited. However, the downside to this level of auditing puts some fairly heavy loads on these systems and often creates instability. The US military has gone to amazing lengths to standardize auditing and system security expectations, as defined by the National Industrial Security PrOgraM (NISPOM), discussed in Chapter 8 (http://www.dss.mil/documents/odaa/nispom2006-5220.pdf).

The healthcare community has been in a Health Insurance Portability and Accountability Act of 1996 (HIPAA) (http://en.wikipedia.org/wiki/Hipaa) security stranglehold, and thin clients have become an essential tool for maintaining patient privacy and medical record security. The lack of swap, cache, or any other sort of long-term local data storage means that stolen or broken workstations don't result in private patient data walking out the door. Layer on group policy control over the use of USB storage devices to really put a kink in someone exporting your data to a portable device (http://support.microsoft.com/kb/555324).

The basic idea is that if you have an intentionally built device that's had all of its general-purpose functions ripped out, then you also have a platform that denies attackers many of the tools that can be typically used against you. VDI means greater control over the workstation image, it means being able to force updates even if the user has powered it off, and it means a greater number of control points for access while still giving users the computing experience they've come to expect.

Chapter 11

Understand Your Cloud Type

The Nature of the Cloud Can Have a Huge Impact on Security Possibilities

Why does the type of cloud matter when it comes to security? It really comes down to how far you can reach into the cloud. Obviously, if you own the cloud the sky is the limit. However, in shared environments there should be fences in place to prevent one user from intruding into a neighbor's resources.

To help understand the various types of clouds, we fall back on terminology that isn't widely used but is, to us, quite helpful. Generically, we see the cloud types as:

- Fully Cloudy—Full abstraction, such as that provided by Amazon and Google. For the most part you do NOT have access to the underlying hypervisor. Unlike the servers in your data center, every machine, switch, disk, and database has a cost associated with it rather than a flat, bundled cost for compute services that you might pay to your IT group. In a fully cloudy environment you might only have the application programming interfaces (APIs) and monitoring provided by the infrastructure provider and, perhaps, monitoring at the server/workstation operating system level for each virtual machine. What you get in return is a highly shared environment that typically has the advantage of being a very small fraction of the real cost of running a fully supported server in a data center. What you give up is access: Getting access to the hypervisor management interface or a fully promiscuous eclectic network interface for auditing may be a considerable additional expense, if it's possible at all.

- Partially Cloudy—Infrastructure as a Service (IaaS): Here the hypervisor itself is the service, and the customer is generally assigned a resource pool to draw upon as they provision systems. IaaS represents a gateway service for many organizations to duplicate systems existing in their data center, in the cloud. The Microsoft® Azure® public cloud has become so closely integrated with Microsoft's Windows Server® that migrating systems between the private cloud (now called Azure Services for Windows Server when hosted in your data center) and the public cloud (Microsoft Azure) has become nearly seamless.

- Privately Cloudy—Here the pundits are in conflict and the market is changing rapidly enough that agreement as to what constitutes the difference between self-service virtualization and private clouds is still evolving. Our opinion is that the self-service component needs to be fully multi-tenant, with the resource pool to include users, servers, networking components, storage, and authentication in order to be a true private cloud.

Clouds Are Bigger Than Organizational Boundaries

We've certainly experienced how easy it has been for project groups to stand up (i.e., create and deploy) a temporary service in the cloud and then tear it down (or abandon it) when the project is done. Is this going to be like that new company coffee doodad? You know the situation, when someone bought the latest and greatest coffee maker and brought it to the office. Once the newness wore off, it was abandoned in the kitchen while everyone went back to regular coffee from the communal pot. Is the new cloud service shared and built upon or does it just disappear one day? Did anyone check for confidential or sensitive information on the abandoned system? Do you have a policy designed to handle this situation?

The answer to any or all of these questions can lead to a promising cloud implementation's abandonment to the wastebin of lost projects.

Cloud services are now so easy to set up that we've seen cloud drives created just so that users can have a way to share storage between workgroups without "meddling" from the IT department, or as a way to bring the road warrior and the home team some shared storage. It's become so easy that we've heard lots of stories (and we're certainly guilty) of forgotten caches of data and cloud services. Did you abandon some of your experiments? Did you forget to delete the data when the "free trial" period was over? Did the "team" forget to delete the data after the project was done, or did you just assume someone else remembered?

We're convinced that users are going to drag resources into the organization no matter what the IT group thinks about this. Just keep in mind that PCs snuck into the business world because users felt that the mainframe folks weren't responding to their needs, and decided to take matters into their own hands. We've certainly gotten a strong sense of *déjà vu* when it comes to the *ad hoc* deployment of cloud services by users instead of the IT group. Our advice is to get ahead of this curve and decide on corporate policy before it gets decided for you. "Bring Your Own Cloud" (BYOC) is already being discussed at major computer industry conferences as a management and security issue. Given the difficulties that many organizations have had with Bring Your Own Device (BYOD) policies, getting in front of the personal cloud issue is critical if companies want to avoid potential security disasters.

Everyone Needs to Agree on the Cloud Under Discussion

Danger, danger! Get ahead of the trend or get buried under it. Sorry to be alarmist, but we're seeing misunderstandings in organizations large and small due to the marketing hype that calls just about anything not locally installed, a cloud app. Much like electricity, users will always follow the path of least resistance. When it comes to clouds, it's certainly easier to stand up a free trial account (and bypass purchasing controls) for something cloudy and then sneak the monthlies into their expense report under donuts than it is to wade through scores of pages (and months of delay) to do things the "right" way.

Are you making the effort to educate your users about clouds, or are you hoping that their ignorance is your bliss? For instance, we've seen many business unit (non-IT department) managers stand up a full server out of ignorance, when in reality they could have gone to a dramatically cheaper SaaS cloud. Or more specifically, you may not need to stand up a full copy of Windows Server® 2016, Microsoft SQL Server®, and Microsoft's Internet Information Services (IIS) at ISP XXX just to get a Drupal™ CMS instance for a team to work on. It might have been more appropriate to stand up a site on a shared Drupal instance at a SaaS provider for a fraction of the cost of the full IaaS site.

The Open Cloud

Although most pieces of the cloud infrastructure are the result of proprietary work and technology, since 2011, cloud builders have had an open source option: OpenStack®. OpenStack is a complete infrastructure for building a cloud. From Swift, a rest-based API for object storage to Keystone, LDAP-compatible ID management, it is possible to create a complete, functional cloud using OpenStack components. OpenStack's promise is for an open source and vendor agnostic cloud solution.

In total, the components of OpenStack are:

- Nova®—Compute
  Nova is a compute fabric controller. As such, it ties many different computing devices into a single, unified cloud resource. Nova can work with both Type 1 and Type 2 hypervisors for virtual machine management.
- Neutron®—Networking
  Since cloud computing involves networking as well as compute resources, it requires dynamic, automated IP address management. That is Neutron's job. In advanced installations, Neutron can be used alongside OpenFlow® for a complete software-defined networking (SDN) implementation.
- Cinder®—Block Storage
  Cinder allows developers to build systems in which users (or their applications) can request and provision block storage for data. These "Cinder blocks" can be persistent, remaining in existence and

accessible even when the specific virtual application instance that created them has ceased to exist. Cinder is particularly useful in a cloud environment because it can create storage blocks that include, and span, many different physical and logical storage types.

- Keystone®—Identity
Securely executing the rest of OpenStack's features requires robust authentication and authorization. Keystone is the OpenStack service that allows for these steps. In addition to providing native token-based authN and user-service authorization and authentication, Keystone allows for use of external authentication and authorization services, as well as oAuth, SAML, and opened.

- Glance®—Image
Normally deployed in conjunction with Keystone, Glance provides an interface for accessing virtual storage and recovery resources.

- Swift®—Object Storage
OpenStack's Cinder communicates with things like iSCSI storage area networks, but Swift stores the objects into block storage. For example, Swift could be used to provide a DropBox®/Box®/Amazon Glacier™–like storage facility. Swift is built for scale and optimized for availability and concurrency across a huge data set. Swift is ideal and most often used for storing unstructured data that can grow without limits.

- Horizon®—Dashboard
Every cloud system needs management, and OpenStack is no different. There are many options for managing an OpenStack implementation, but Horizon is the canonical ("official") management interface of the OpenStack project. Horizon collects the management features and functions into a unified web interface comprising three central dashboards—a "User," "System," and "Settings." Between these three, they cover the core OpenStack applications. Horizon also ships with a set of API abstractions for the core Open-Stack projects.

- Heat®—Orchestration
This is where the promise of OpenStack begins to be fulfilled. Instead of being forced to deploy OpenStack as a series of individual services, Heat allows you to manage the OpenStack pieces as a collection. Fortunately for administrators and managers, Heat manages

both the individual components of OpenStack and the relationships between the pieces.

- Mistral®—Workflow
Mistral is an automation piece for workflows of nearly any kind, though it is frequently used to automate the process of creating OpenStack instances. Descriptions of the work flow are uploaded into Mistral, which can then take care of scheduling, order of execution, process state monitoring, managing parallel execution, and much more.

- Ceilometer®—Telemetry
Ceilometer is the OpenStack infrastructure for providing telemetry data to management and monitor applications. Although Ceilometer began as a project to make billing for services possible, it grew to incorporate the features for providing any sort of data to management applications. Ceilometer is the heart of the OpenStack operations center, providing the infrastructure to support metering, monitoring, and alerting for all OpenStack services.

- Trove®—Database
Trove is the Database as a Service (DBaaS) component of the OpenStack universe. Although you can certainly provision a full SQL server to handle your data storage needs, Trove provides for much simpler relational or non-relational database storage needs. Trove will not serve every database need for an enterprise; it is not a replacement for Oracle®, DB2®, or any of the other major relational database managers for enterprise applications. If the requirement is for a database that handles monitoring and management tasks, though, Trove is a serious contender.

- Sahara®—Elastic Map Reduce
This used to be called Savanna but potential trademark issues forced a name change. Sahara is designed to be the deployment and management engine behind Hadoop instances on OpenStack. If you're planning on running a "Big Data" system under OpenStack, you will more than likely be dealing with Sahara to manage the provisioning.

- Ironic®—Bare Metal
Although most OpenStack instances will live on virtual or cloud operating system platforms, there are use cases that require a standalone, bare-metal server sitting under the OpenStack deployment. These cases are the reason that Ironic was developed. Sometimes

thought of as a fork of Nova, Ironic is a specialized thin hypervisor typically used for handling on-demand or on-the-fly provisioning for handling emerging loads.

- Zaqar®—Messaging
  Although certainly not a copy of the Amazon SQS messaging API, Zaqar is designed to be a RESTFul API to pass messages between applications in a firewall/proxy/load balancer friendly methodology and rests heavily on the foundation built by Amazon SQS. Zaqar has its roots in research done in early high-performance computing clusters such as the Beowulf MPI (message passing interface). Cloud OpenStack operators frequently built services on top of Zaqar to provide SQS and SNS equivalents to their customers.

- Manila®—Shared File System
  It is tough to say what Manila will look like in production because at the time of this writing it exists as a proposal for a shared storage capability between OpenStack compute instances. One potential use case might look like this: Neutron is deployed in a load balancer as a service configuration in front of a number of Nova instances running a public web presence. The content to populate the web pages could be stored in Manila, with Trove being used for transaction storage. The entire instance would, of course, be deployed using a Mistral workflow.

- Designate®—DNS
  Designate is a domain name service designed for a multi-tenant environment. It has identity connections to OpenStack Keystone. It is easy to imagine how handy this could be as systems such as DNS DANE,[1] where users would authenticate against Keystone and have encryption keys handed to them by DANE. Imagine being able to have trusted web sites with trusted encryption keys handed out by the owner of the domain, aka the DNS authority.

- Searchlight®—Search
  The online world lives and dies by search, and what this OpenStack piece provides is controllable search across a multi-tenant system by offloading much of the indexing into Elasticsearch.

- Barbican®—Key Manager
  This key manager is a RESTful interface for the management of passwords, X.509 certificates, and provides an interface for securing resources within the OpenStack environment. Although this may

sound like a certificate authority, Barbican was designed to do much more, especially as resources such as DNS Dane become ratified by the Internet Engineering Task Force (IETF).

- TBD—Extensibility
  The key to OpenStack's success so far is its extensibility. It's quite likely that by the time this book hits the bookstores, this list of OpenStack key pieces will be out of date. What we're hoping is that OpenStack will by then migrate out of the lab and into the front line enough to get the big players to start adopting this future.

What OpenStack really does is provide a common API set, management, metering, and alerting platform that seeks to make cloud computing truly agnostic. Since you can install OpenStack and its resources on Amazon Web Services®, Microsoft® Azure®, RackSpace®, and other cloud and physical platforms, what you gain from this extra abstraction layer is the commonality of the OpenStack environment, regardless of the platform.

Not surprisingly, OpenStack has also grown to include three pieces of software that contribute directly to the security of the project. Anchor, Bandit, and Syntribos each play a role in OpenStack security and will be covered in an upcoming chapter.

We predicted in our first book, *Cloud Computing: Technologies and Strategies of the Ubiquitous Data Center*,[2] that the future of cloud computing would be sufficiently reduced to a commodity basis for its various components that customers would be able to shop around for "discounted resources" to run scheduled peak computing tasks (e.g., payroll, invoicing, etc.). It is our belief that this future is fast approaching, and although OpenStack isn't ubiquitous yet, it's gaining ground fast enough that the vast majority of the players have it running in their development labs.

References

1. Žorž, J. (2017, Sept.). "DNS Over TLS: Experience from the Go6lab." Internet Society. Accessed December 26, 2017, from https://www.internetsociety.org/blog/2017/09/dns-tls-experience-go6lab/
2. Chee, Brian J. S. and Franklin, C., Jr. (2010). *Cloud Computing: Technologies and Strategies of the Ubiquitous Data Center*, 1st Edition. Boca Raton, FL: CRC Press.

Chapter 12

Public Cloud

Classic Clouds Are Public

It was through the Amazon Elastic Compute Cloud™ (Amazon EC2™) that many first heard the term "cloud computing." There is no doubt that the world is changing and that, for much of the general public, clouds no longer just describe meteorological phenomena. Putting aside some fairly lame television commercials, the general public is certainly equating clouds as good things for saving family photos; and cloud storage services such as Dropbox®, OneDrive®, and Google Drive™ have become de rigueur for the typical mobile user.

People have been using back-end compute clouds hidden behind flashy interfaces for services such as "Siri®," Google Maps™/Google Translate™/ etc., and even Dragon® Dictate (which does the bulk of the heavy lifting for voice dictation, using a back-end cloud service). There is now enough differentiation for cloud storage that Amazon now has Glacier™, at a dramatically less-expensive pricing scheme, which is targeted at backup and archiving, while sacrificing frequent retrieval.

So although backup and storage is how the general public view clouds, the big advantages are for applications and their ability to change size and capabilities on the fly. What keeps the pricing for all these application types under control is how Amazon, Microsoft, and Google all provide key systems features in a lower-overhead flavor instead of forcing you to run full-size databases, transcoding, and messaging servers.

In a nutshell, what all the public cloud vendors are doing is providing critical services such as database, messaging, caching, and web applications in a stripped-down fashion. Amazon Web Services™ (AWS™) actually calls their shared database "Amazon DynamoDB™," which provides SQL-like database services without the cost of paying to host a full-size SQL server. As with similar offerings from Google and Microsoft, the key here is that customers only pay for what they use. Part of the allure of such services is that, in general, temporary surges are lost in the noise, and payments are normally made by the amount of I/O and the amount of data stored at a certain time of day when accounting is done. Services on a similar model are available for inter-virtual (inter-VM) machine communications and messaging.

So, although all these services are nice, the security question becomes, Just how private are they really? Although the various service providers tend to keep the specifics of their infrastructure obscured, our best guess is that Amazon's DynamoDB is a really big database server set up for multi-tenancy: Anyone who manages to snag account login information could potentially use those credentials to execute unauthorized queries directly against the database and through those queries gain access to sensitive information. Obviously, the advantage to this sort of architecture is cost, since customers are only paying a small fraction of the total cost of running a full-size database server with the associated costs of virtual machines and licensing for one or more database managers.

From the customer perspective, it's even better that these building block services are highly scalable. As long as a customer is willing to pay for increased capacity, they could potentially span the globe using global load-balancing services to direct users to the nearest physical data center location. That very attractive capability brings up more to think about in terms of securing this new scalable system. How is the interprocess communication (IPC) set up? Are these communications secure? What are the risks involved to both data and processes?

To answer these questions, we take some concepts from the Amazon website with the caveat that these commitments are fairly generic and common to just about every public cloud service we've dealt with.

Amazon notes that all messages are stored in a redundant format across multiple sites and systems. The complexity of that redundancy is largely hidden from developers, who need to use only five application programming interfaces (APIs) to create a message queue and manipulate the messages in and out of that queue. An additional advantage of the Amazon method is its affordable scaling, requiring no up-front payments, instead relying on a per-request transfer and handling fee.

We mention AWS specifically because it's very much like named pipes (with all their advantages and disadvantages): Although it gives you the ability to pass messages between AWS-based applications [or between different data centers with Amazon Simple Notification Service™ (SNS™)], it does add another place where potentially vulnerable data can sit. This kind of communications system tends to place quite a bit of trust in the application, and thus should be something for which you change credentials on a regular basis. Those credentials should change immediately (within minutes, if possible), if a person of trust leaves your organization.

If we were to wax paranoid for a bit, we might imagine a situation in which a person of trust leaves the organization and accidentally takes some of those certificates/credentials home with them. It wouldn't be too far-fetched for them to set up a free AWS "trial" account and insert the purloined credentials. The lesson? Don't forget to change application credentials at the same time you change the admin passwords.

We bring this up because AWS (and its messaging component) are often overlooked and are key parts of breaking cloud apps into scalable pieces. Much of the basic architectural design for this type of service is based upon research done in the high-performance computing (HPC) world where the capability is called a message-passing interface (MPI). The critical architectural point is that there is a master node that then spawns additional slave nodes to work on individual pieces of the program.

It's the master node's responsibility to collect the results through MPI and fit together the puzzle pieces. A high level of trust between these nodes is a given. Another is that, when depending upon administrator setup timers, these messages could potentially sit for day or weeks while systems wait on timers to expire. It's easy to believe that the collegial world of HPC computing tends not to worry about long-duration data and connections, but this is a case in which academia offers lessons to the enterprise.

A best practice from the MPI world is to make sure you have a cleanup function that also cleans up external MPIs and the resulting messages sitting around in the queue. As with user credentials and legally discoverable email messages, understanding the importance of sweeping away data when its usefulness has ended is critical to maintain security in cloud services.

Have you heard the story about a service company that was upgrading desktop machines for a client? You know, the service company that then held onto the old hard disks and sold them to the customer's competitor? This story illustrates the concept that data—even on powered-down and retired machines—potentially contains proprietary information, which is why we bring up the next concept that has gained significant traction in the enterprise IT world.

"Encrypt in place" means that all sensitive information is stored on an encrypted volume so that even when that server is powered down, that data has a degree of safety. We wouldn't be so bold as to say safe, especially in a world-accessible cloud system, but safer than if we used a standard unencrypted volume.

Microsoft has been a frequent leader in understanding enterprise needs, and the "Encrypted File System" (EFS) is a great case in point. This standard feature of the Windows® operating system (both workstation and server) allows you to encrypt individual files, folders, or entire volumes, and is compatible with services such as the Amazon Elastic Block Store™ (EBS™).[1]

In this case, when you create a new volume on Microsoft® Azure®/ AWS/etc., you simply check the "EFS" box and follow the instructions. The process for Linux® distributions is a bit different. However, while it requires a few more steps, the final result is the same.[2] Putting our "paranoia cap" on for a bit, it's not such a stretch to copy a volume off and then mount it on another machine where you already have root access. When this happens, the data is decrypted on the "read" operation and placed on the target drive in an unencrypted state. Why encrypt, if that's the case? Encrypting in place at least makes the bad guys suck up a ton of compute time to try to break the encryption, which hopefully then gives you enough time to mitigate the damage that data loss could potentially cause.

The conclusion a person might want to take away from this chapter is that wherever data sits, it's vulnerable. Even if you have a service-level agreement (SLA) saying that the cloud provider is going to protect your data, the reality is that the provider is only going to put out the effort defined by the SLA. So perhaps you, as a customer, might want to go the few extra steps so as to not tempt fate. Encrypting and changing keys/ credentials for programs as well as users, along with encrypting in place, could make a cloud just as safe as your internal data center.

Each Cloud Provider Is Unique

Like anything in life, the advantages of size depend upon what you want out of the entity in question. Life in a small town means that you know everyone there, but it also means that any indiscretion is known to the entire town very quickly. The same goes for cloud providers. A smaller single-city provider means that you probably will get a higher touch value with them, but it also means that if you want something like global load balancing you may need to bring in a third party. It's really about managing your expectations, and realizing that nothing comes for free. So, let's look at some typical cloud-deployment scenarios and try to imagine what services you really need versus those that would be convenient but won't greatly affect the functionality of your system.

The Network Connecting Customer and Cloud Is Key to Both Security and Performance

One huge change to the cloud computing market is marked by the speed with which vendors are implementing software-defined networking (SDN) as part of their cloud architecture. Unfortunately, this rush to change has spawned a large number of incompatible cloud and network variations. Someday, we may see gateways to convert between competing "standards." Perhaps the Institute of Electrical and Electronics Engineers (IEEE) and the Internet Engineering Task Force (IETF) will reach agreement on a true industry standard for SDN. Until that blessed day, let's just look at what Microsoft is doing in their Windows® Server 2012 R2 offering and how Microsoft might eventually be the driving force for a functional multivendor integration standard.

It's no secret that the network market wants a secure standard to extend organizational networks to the cloud and provide a secure link to branch offices without the complexity of VLAN tunneling over VPNs. It should also be noted that, at time of writing, no industry standard exists for SDNs, although some vendors claim "standard" victory in a market that really hasn't even started yet. However, with a huge part of the market running on Microsoft® Windows® Server technology, one might make a prediction that the Microsoft solution and potential for cross-"standard" integration could logically be the glue necessary for integration.

For instance, an organization could set up an AWS link to the home office through a VPN, while using the Cisco® SDN solution to link to their branch offices. That same gateway server could also run portions of the OpenStack® system to link to a newly acquired company that went that route. Although not intended to act like a router, Windows Server has had that capability for decades, and has also recently added WAN routing in the form of Border Gateway Protocol (BGP) to bridge internal routing (perhaps Open Shortest Path First [OSPF]) to their upstream ISP using BGP. The fact that the connection strings look just like SSL URLs would have one believe that perhaps the intervening WAN technology will soon no longer matter.

The key advantage over traditional VPNs is how you can link various sites together, even if they have potentially conflicting addressing and/or routing schemes. So the paradigm change here is that instead of concentrating on traditional VLAN trunking, the center of the network is typically visualized as a cloud. With the SDN core and network devices handling inter-device communications, the edge devices can make the virtual networks appear on demand. It should be pointed out that SDN is one of those technologies that has gradually appeared and, for the most part, is based upon proprietary solutions by large networking vendors for reducing the configuration and maintenance headache of large VLAN-based networks.

The true future of clouds is a gradual move toward greater amounts of abstraction in how you provide services. Microsoft's demos have even gone as far as having servers with conflicting addressing being dropped into a cloud and having the base infrastructure solve the conflicts for you. One of the most ignored cloud features is how Microsoft has integrated "Azure Services for Windows Server 2012 R2" to allow for live migration of virtual services from the private to public clouds based upon business rules.

In Provider Relationships, Service-Level Agreements (SLAs) Rule

SLAs begin with making sure you understand your organization's needs versus wants. Asking for the moon may make you look great in front of your management, but the hosting service may charge you more to add that feature and then just pay the penalties instead of making the large investment to fulfill an unreasonable item in your SLA. A good strategy is to create a realistic two-column list of needs and wants. What do you need to meet your business requirements, and what do you want to enable expansion? These lists need to be in hand before you go shopping for the SLA, so that your requests have a chance to stay within the realm of reality.

Do you really need SDN in the cloud now, or can you afford to work with your vendor to implement this feature in a future expansion? If you need it, perhaps this is something you can co-develop with them as a partnership to lower initial costs and still fulfill that "need" in the nearer future. In a project at the University of Hawaii, we ran into a set of functions that was high on the wish list but wouldn't need to be on the need list for at least a couple of years. The advantage of waiting was that we could partner with the vendor to develop a better-fit solution and didn't end up having to pay for any custom coding. We're still not quite able to have full Active Directory® federation with open LDAP, but we're close enough that we can start budgeting for it.

Dynamic Provisioning and Capacity Flexibility Must Be Covered in the SLA

One of the better kept secrets of the old mainframe service bureaus was the ability to use fairly large amounts of scratch space; if you cleaned up the temp files before midnight, you didn't have to pay for the additional memory use. Although not quite that forgiving, temp areas are part and parcel of many cloud systems in the form of surge allowances. You can surge past your allotment as long as that surge drops to expected levels before the billing period. One cloud trick that we've rarely seen is language in the SLA that handles how you calculate overall disk usage and how you handle modern de-duplication technology. Do you use real storage or storage indicated by total metadata? The difference can be large and critical.

Calculating real storage costs versus rack space is another possibility that some vendors allow for. It could potentially be cheaper to separate your storage into layers: online, near-line, and offline. Do you need a petabyte of past accounting data in expensive fast storage? Perhaps it would be more reasonable to have a rack of slower SATA-based near-line arrays to make those records available, but on slower, less-expensive storage. You might even consider optical jukeboxes for long-term storage. Metadata not only stays on the system for searching but also will trigger a retrieval from optical storage based upon another set of access rules.

Customer Data Security Should Be Governed by the SLA

Just how are backups stored, and what are the provider's access rules? What happens to data on a drive that goes bad and is swapped out? What we're talking about here is where sensitive data's value can potentially far outstrip the value of the systems it's stored upon. Both Dell™ and HP® now have standard line items that allow for replacement drives to be provided, while leaving the defective drives with the customer for proper disposal.

These represent good questions about data at rest, but just what measures should you take yourself or in cooperation with the vendor to protect data in transit? There is a VERY good reason why telecommunications centers such as cable-landing sites and central/switching offices are what Homeland Security calls strategic resources. The ability to covertly insert monitoring systems between the source and destination has long been a subject of concern by security experts. The fact that man-in-the-middle devices and network taps can be nearly undetectable under certain circumstances makes it increasingly important to ask the vendor what their clearance standards are for employees, guests, and contractors.

Data Must Be Secure at Every Point in the Transaction

While we beat this subject to death, we should point out that the difference between network monitoring and diagnostic and hacking tools is basically intent. So it becomes an item to ask your provider about who's watching the watchers and what kinds of background checks are performed on personnel who have access to this kind of infrastructure.

Getting down to brass tacks, sending encrypted traffic down an encrypted tunnel may sound like a waste of bandwidth and computing power, but what it does is remove places where misplaced trust could burn you. There is also a saying that during WWII, even highly sensitive correspondence was sent via the US Postal Service because spies would then have to look at all the US Postal correspondence and not just the letter that stood out because of special handling. The same goes for data; if everything is encrypted, what do you spend your computing time on decrypting? If you create sub-pipes of encrypted data, then the decrypting problem goes up exponentially. So, for example, a VPN between sites is normal, but sensitive human resources (HR) data is further encrypted and then sent down the "normal pipe."

Cloud Provider Demise Must Be Covered in the SLA

Some of the items you need to add to your need list is what you imagine you would need if key personnel become unavailable or what your needs are if your vendor closes its doors. What happens when there's a situation like that of Nirvanix®? When a cloud service provider closes their doors, where does your data go and who's responsible for scrubbing the physical drives (http://www.infoworld.com/d/virtualization/cloud-storage-provider-nirvanix-closing-its-doors-227289)?

While we don't like advocating putting in backdoors to your systems, we've used several systems just to make sure we don't get locked out of our own systems when the admin goes on vacation or is in an accident. Something as simple as a procedure to always write down the new password, seal it in an envelope, and lock it away with someone is about as simple as it comes. Just make sure your operations manual AND employee handbook include procedures for business continuity by making sure that no one person can lock you out if they're unavailable for some reason. Brian is fond of encrypted password vaults and computer-generated passwords. The master password to the vault is kept with a trusted third party and only released if the system administrator becomes incapacitated. This also means that the encrypted vault can be backed up to cloud storage with a reasonable expectation that it won't become public.

This type of procedure has become even more important as server technology transitions from the decades old BIOS (basic input output system) to the new universal extensible firmware interface (UEFI; http://www.uefi.org/) that, among other features, allows for encrypted disk volumes. So if those disks or copies get moved to another server, they become unusable. This also means that in order to import other disks into your EUFI system, you need that password. What happens if this is at a service provider? Or worse yet, in a shared virtual environment? What procedures has your provider put into place to make sure that the UEFI credentials aren't lost if they lose key personnel?

References

1. "Encrypting File System." (2012). docs.microsoft.com. Accessed December 26, 2017, from https://docs.microsoft.com/en-us/previous-versions/windows/it-pro/windows-vista/cc749610(v=ws.10)
2. "How Do I Create an Encrypted Filesystem Inside a File?" (2017). askubuntu.com. Accessed December 26, 2017, from https://askubuntu.com/questions/58935/how-do-i-create-an-encrypted-filesystem-inside-a-file

Chapter 13

Private Cloud

Private Clouds Start with Virtualization

Although cloud foundations lie in the world of virtualization, it is in resource abstraction that a collection of virtual hosts becomes a cloud. It is also this abstraction that will form the future of cloud technology and how the market must eventually achieve true systems agnostics. Someday in the near future we should not care that the cloud is VMWare®-, Microsoft®-, or Linux®-based, but we should care about the toolsets offered by the cloud vendor. We are certainly getting closer, as vendors such as Amazon don't even mention VMWare until you dig very deeply into their documentation, nor does their "normal" Amazon Web Services™ (AWS™) offering even allow you any kind of view into the base OS. The fact that more and more organizations are adopting system agnostic content management systems—for example, Drupal™, Joomla!®, and their ilk—only proves that the world doesn't seem to care what's under the hood. They just care that they can get their tasks done, just as the vast majority of people in the world only marginally cares what brand of car they drive. Most consumers really only care that it gets them where they want to go, when they want to get there, and for a cost they can afford. So although the marketing teams at Microsoft, VMWare, and RedHat® would like you to believe that each is much better than its competitors, the marketing horse race is doing a fairly good job of getting all vendors to copy the features announced by one, thus yielding specification sheets nearly interchangeable between vendors.

Our entirely unscientific speculation is that someday portability between systems will become expected to the point at which someone could actually go comparative shopping for a cloud vendor (see Chapter 11 on OpenStack®). Our brand of science fiction that we hope to become science fact is a scenario in which a contractor may want to figure out wind load on a beach home they're building. They should be able to purchase the use of the same system a mega architectural firm uses to do similar calculations on a skyscraper, all by shopping the offerings from cloud vendors. Today, this is very much a "George Jetson"–level dream for the future, but there is no reason why it can't someday become reality.

The scenario leading the pack is that of a hybrid solution where organizational computing is done with a mix of more traditional private clouds to handle on-demand surges into the public cloud based upon business rules. At the time of writing, the most common hybrid scenario is where prototyping is done within the confines of a private data center where localized resources are at hand and costs of running multiple versions of the system under development are less of a worry. This type of scenario also provides a way to temporarily ignore some of the security issues in favor of getting the systems working, after which the tuning process can then include closing up the vulnerabilities. Another advantage is that while the system is being fine-tuned, the organization has better control over operational costs and access to the organizational diagnostic systems for security and performance. This public+private hybrid also brings surge capabilities wherein usage statistics can trigger business rules for "spinning up" additional virtualized copies of the system(s) and/or allocating additional virtual resources to handle surges. A great example of this is when an organization makes an announcement that catches the public's eye and gets posted to a service like Slashdot Media® or a news story on CNN®. The sudden and massive traffic surge could potentially drive a huge sales spike, but only if your web system can rise to the occasion. In this case, it has become common to keep mirrors of key web systems synchronized between public and private cloud instances so that demand can trigger activation of those public mirrors. Through load balancing, the surge can be balanced between public and private clouds, or, through global load balancing, the load can be shifted to cloud facilities physically closer to the demand. Since you only pay for what you use, it's much easier to justify the extra capabilities to corporate finance departments.

Difference between Virtualization and Private Cloud Comes Down to Self-Service Provisioning and Dynamic Capacity Adjustment

We keep saying clouds are about abstraction to the point at which computing becomes a commodity. This commoditization will only happen if as few humans as possible need to the touch the process. So in a way, self-service also needs to happen, and on a scale never before seen in the IT world. The audience at the Microsoft rollout of Server 2012 nearly came to their feet when the Microsoft Server and Tools division announced Azure® Services for Windows Server 2012 R2 and it's ability to provide self-service systems provisioning in your own data center. The key to "self-service" is for more of the resource allocation to be available to project groups as a pool that can be drawn upon as needed. Templates of pre-defined organizational resources translate to workgroups being able to spin up a customer relationship management (CRM) system with all the associated pieces (i.e., IIS with SQL backend and secure connections to the organizational SQL) mostly predefined. Instead of deploying a single server at a time, the self-service system allows workgroups to deploy an entire system that has already been vetted by the IT group. From a security standpoint, the concept of pre-vetted configurations mean that, in theory, those workgroups also start off with far fewer vulnerabilities and far more best-practices already implemented. The promise of systems being tested instead of just clicking defaults should go a very long way in preventing huge attack surfaces for hackers to exploit.

The monkey wrench in the works is, simply put, latency and jitter over the distances between the cloud data centers. Expecting to be able to transfer a fresh virtual machine or cloud app over the wide area network fast enough to meet surge demand isn't reality quite yet. With the current limitations of the global backbone, cloud engineers have instead worked on systems to periodically synchronize apps and server images—either periodically during the day or during off-peak periods. One of the classic questions governed by how fast you can synchronize those databases or even if you need to is, How often? If we're talking about an e-commerce sales cycle, perhaps a couple of hours delay in pricing updates might not be earth shattering, but we're sure stocking levels might be. As with any large-scale endeavor, the answer isn't black and white but many shades of the rainbow.

The increase in cloud infrastructure and network complexity has been accompanied by a trend in the IT industry toward a more specialized and compartmentalized work force. Generalization has certainly fallen out of favor at universities, as it has at most large organizations. The "kids" can't lean on the "old timers" as they slowly retire, and big-picture skills aren't being replaced. The fact is that more and more organizations are looking to outsourcing design functions to contractors, thus robbing the younger employees of the chance at learning those big-picture skills.

Getting more to the point, clouds are the proverbial double-edged sword in that they can make science fiction–like promises, but will require extra care in making sure niggling little details—for instance, the laws of physics—aren't ignored. Let's look at an example of an arms race between monster cruise ship lines. It seems a big differentiator for cruise ships is the quality of their passenger Internet connection while at sea. The knee-jerk reaction is that just paying more for faster satellite connections would be the answer; but the owners of one of the new super cruise ships discovered that faster off-ship connections are only a small part of the solution. What is apparent is that the flood of user expectations quickly overwhelmed even the upgraded satellite connections, gaining the owners a huge amount of negative press from disappointed passengers. This could have been predicted by a team that understood how all the systems work (i.e., generalists) and was willing to confirm marketing claims instead of blindly believing sales claims. If we were to attempt to fill that team's shoes, we'd have to beg, borrow, or steal a traffic simulation system—for example, one from Spirent or Ixia—and then model all the ship's traffic over a link degradation tool, such as the Maxwell® by InterWorking Labs® (http://iwl.com/).

In this example we might use the Maxwell to simulate the latency and jitter found on satellite links and "tune" key apps like proxies and caches in order to reduce factors like latency-driven retransmission. The reason for this tuning is that most browsers and network stacks will often attempt a TCP retransmission before the acknowledgment has a chance to make the round trip on a congested satellite link. In a similar situation, a cloud application team willing to test the full architecture can prevent some network clogging from spurious retransmission requests with proxies and caches.

The proxy in this example would be "tuned" to accommodate the longer transmission times. Another key is to cache an organization's most-used destinations—for example, their mission-critical enterprise applications—so that only the first request in a given time period would reach across the satellite link, with each subsequent request being serviced from the local cache. Portions of the web page that change will, of course, need to be retrieved each time, but items such as logos, frames, contact information, and so forth, which hardly ever change, can be cached with potentially huge bandwidth savings.

While the cruise ship example is extreme, it does point out that the laws of physics can't be ignored. For the moment, it is in your best interest to make sure that you understand where your globally load-balanced site is in relation to your potential customers. The moral of this story is: Get a bigger picture and confirm that view of the world with testing.

Cloud Implies Geographic Dispersal, but There Are Critical Exceptions

Widespread geographic dispersal of your computing resources into the cloud just sounds like a great idea. No single outage of a communications path or data center can take you off the air. Instead, city blackouts or brownouts remain news items rather than critical disasters for you. However, geographic dispersal also needs to be balanced with where your customers/users are. The big picture is all about perspective. We would speculate that one of the reasons why Amazon's Glacier™ backup solution is so inexpensive is that Amazon is able to utilize usage patterns to optimize where and when they synchronize your backup data in that secondary or tertiary backup location as per the service-level agreement (SLA). So while you might have your home base in the Eastern United States, you may just end up doing a restore from a European data center. In this case, Amazon is making use of less-used facilities to lower your cost, but if you have some regulations about where you data can be stored, then you have a problem—not the least of which is that doing a restore from Europe instead of the United States is probably going to take longer if you're located in the Eastern United States.

Global dispersal of your computing assets also means that you're more than likely expecting to be able to shift your load around between cloud facilities for things such as maintenance, surges, or disasters. This is where you need to dust off your calculator and make sure that you're able to synchronize that last little bit of data within your management's expectation for failovers. Is this time to do a test run? What happens if someone does a denial-of-service (DoS) attack? Are your cloud images encrypted? Although these questions sound a bit disjointed, they all pertain to how fast you can move data, and how fast you can get that data into a useful form. Let's tear these issues apart and ask a few questions along the way about whether new vulnerabilities have been introduced.

First, ask the most basic of questions: Just how sensitive is your data? We're both BIG fans of encrypting, and we both consider organizational data to be among an organization's most valuable assets. Unless you're paying for some truly spectacular data pipes within your organization, the first large block of data your organization moves into the cloud is probably going to travel on removable storage of some sort. Does this need to be encrypted, and can your cloud vendor handle an encrypted removable volume? Next, synchronization needs to happen to keep your data stores current. Are those synchronization pathways trustworthy, and do you need to encrypt them? When nation states throw their resources behind cyber attacks, they also tend to have patience. There is a saying that some of our enemies are patient and willing to collect grains of sand. Do that long enough and pretty soon you have your own beach. Can someone steal a copy of your organization's critical data with a tap, SPAN port, or a man-in-the-middle machine at your ISP? You may also want to ask yourself: Who can get to those cloud images, and what kinds of permissions do they need to launch the imaged applications? Can someone tap off your synchronization images, put together a complete system, and then launch it without credentials? Speaking of credentials, self-service also means you've made a few trust compromises as you delegate the right to launch cloud-hosted systems. Have you taken as much care on those delegated trusts as on your in-house directory authentication systems? If you're taking advantage of the emerging capabilities for self-service, can that trust be broken, thus leaving you open to someone exporting a copy of a key system when they spin up a "departmental" copy of your CRM? Although we're not saying that this cloud feature is inherently bad, we are advocating acknowledging the potential for abuse and are encouraging folks to at least make sure they do a reasonable amount of auditing and logging of potentially sensitive areas.

Working our way outward, you should ask whether your upstream ISP has taken reasonable measures to prevent unauthorized interceptions of your data stream. Although the United States has long considered switching centers to be of strategic value, what about other countries? Encryption inherently has overhead associated with it, and we seriously doubt that even the major service providers in the world of clouds are encrypting all their traffic. We would certainly hope that if you ask for it, at least medium to large cloud providers can make encryption part of your SLA, if you need it.

On the other hand, let's look at this in a slightly different manner. The instances of data being intercepted during transmission are relatively rare, and if you read carefully, you'll find that most of the big data breaches are when the data is at rest. So maybe we need to consider encrypting the data at rest, and make sure that we don't make it easy to reach outside of authorized pathways. There has been a major push by all the virtualization systems (Microsoft, VMWare, etc.) to provide support for encrypted volumes (UEFI is a good example[1]) and improved encrypted remote access technologies to link users to their cloud instances. So perhaps, instead of relying upon the cloud vendor to charge you for encrypted pipes for data synchronization, maybe you could utilize the encryption integrated into essentially every modern operating system. So as long as you're staying in the world of Infrastructure as a Service (IaaS; where you actually see the operating system), and you do have control over the base operating system (OS), then you could, for instance, create an encrypted pipe between the home office and cloud instances for database synchronization.

But what options are available as we move closer to true clouds, in architectures such as Applications as a Service, where you no longer see the base OS? To answer this, we're grabbing a bit from an overview document from Amazon. In this case, they think that data security is important enough that they're claiming to meet or exceed US Federal Government regulations on data security (FISMA) and ". . . in accordance with the Risk Management Framework (RMF) process defined in NIST 800-37 and DoD Information Assurance Certification and Accreditation Process (DIACAP) . . ."[2] So although all of this is quite reassuring, it also needs to be backed up by policies and procedures to keep access methods secure and trusted.

To say that the Single Sign-On (SSO) market is white hot is probably a gross understatement. Just about every security vendor on earth is chasing the holy grail of creating a system in which your users only need to authenticate once, while the SSO system handles behind the scenes authentication and trust exchange on systems the user is authorized to access. This is an area in which a huge amount of work is happening and where we think there is the potential to close a huge number of vulnerabilities in modern networked systems. Make it so that users stop using Post-It® notes and simple passwords, and make it so that strong encryption and strong authentication systems are easy to use, and perhaps we can close up the vast majority of the social hacks we suffer through today. Shoulder surfing a password by a faux delivery person shouldn't work, nor should key loggers. The concept of something you know and something you have for multifactor authentication (MFA) combined with modern SSO systems could potentially remove a huge number of intrusion tools for the modern hacker.

What needs to happen is a systematic inventory and securing of the ways to get at your data and sensitive systems. Encrypt at rest, encrypt your access methods, and work toward eliminating the Achilles' heel of modern security systems—humans and passwords.

The Security Issues of Virtualization Apply to Private Clouds, Although They Are Amplified by Self-Service Provisioning and Dynamic Capacity Adjustment

We spoke about knowing your risks during delegation and how you should at least understand where a major theft of critical data could leave your organization. Virtualization means that an exact copy of your systems could potentially be copied onto removable storage, and with snapshot facilities on modern virtualization systems, that can happen without shutting down any system or application. Self-service copies of entire systems have made this process even easier since, in the case of the software-defined networking (SDN) inside modern cloud systems, you can literally create and run an exact system copy, right down to the networking infrastructure.

Since we're spinning a yarn about potential ways to steal critical data, let's take this horror story just a bit further. We spoke about why switching centers for ISPs are considered to be a strategic asset by most governments since, previously, tapping a communication path required physical access. That's no longer true since the advent of virtual taps and virtual remote monitoring systems. If just anyone can spin up a virtual machine, it also means that just anyone can launch a data capture appliance that potentially could intercept data coming to/from your virtual servers—all without stepping foot in the physical data center. So let's share a bit of bad news and reiterate that just hitting enter on a default value during an installation could easily leave a massive vulnerability behind. So let's examine how a default installation value can come back and bite you.

What most professionals know, and what most professionals tend to not have time to implement, is a greater level of granularity in just who can modify things like virtual switches and networks. Microsoft and VMWare both provide the widgets to delegate authority to sub-administrators defining who can modify the SDN that is now available in nearly all the hypervisor systems on the market today. These systems could potentially have an SDN administrator who can create the intersystem links AND set up which of the virtual switches are isolated or have external access. So best practices could be imagined where the network team has vetted the organizational SDN, and you no longer have the need to let your sub-teams use the full administrator credentials. The point we're making is that modern virtualization systems allow you to carve off sub-administrators; perhaps it's time you took advantage of this capability. If you can't modify the SDN, then you can't add a remote probe or tap.

Questions Are Only Now Beginning to Be Resolved around Software Licensing Issues

Although a bit of a side topic, licensing needs to be part of any conversation on clouds and virtualization, in general. Just because a system can run in a virtualized environment, doesn't mean it's legal. A great example is Apple's OS X® Server, which has been able to run under most modern hypervisors, but, according to the Apple End User license agreement, is NOT a legal instance unless it's running on Apple hardware. Another good example is AutoCAD®, which was only legal to virtualize as of the 2012 release, and then only with certain versions. Another licensing hidden danger is how the vast majority of commercial networked applications handle their licensing with systems such as FlexLM™ now called FlexPublisher™ by Globetrotter, Inc.,[3] to manage their so-called "floating licenses."

Some IT Professionals Now Question Whether Virtualization Will Inevitably Evolve Toward the Cloud

Every single conversation we've had in regard to whether an organization should move one or more services into the cloud revolved around money. The question of whether to maintain your own data center and the human resources necessary to manage those resources is always part of the conversation on whether a move to the cloud is warranted. The real Achilles' heel of clouds actually has become how dependent they've all become on Dynamic Name Systems (DNS) and the October 21, 2016, DoS attack on the Dyn Corporation domain-naming systems.[4] This particular attack didn't really attack the websites but rather the general public's ability to get to them. Interestingly enough, if you knew the actual IP address of the website, you could still get them. However, because so many of the web pages contain hundreds of other web components that all use names instead of IP addresses, we were able to get a portion of the web site's front page, but with hundreds of broken links.

Here's a summary of the Mirai distributed denial-of-service (DDoS) Botnet attack on Dyn DNS from a presentation done by Cricket Liu of Infoblox Inc.:

- Hurled traffic at Dyn's name servers
  - Said to peak at **1.2 Tbps**
  - Unclear whether it was junk traffic (e.g., SYN, GRE) or legitimate DNS queries
  - Name servers rendered unresponsive
- High-profile Dyn customers impacted
  - A.K.A., the Web

The answer according to the InfoBlox presentation is Response Rate Limiting:

- Originally a patch to BIND 9 by Paul Vixie and Vernon Schryver
  - Now included in BIND 9, other name servers
- Applies to authoritative name servers used in DDoS attacks against others
- Prevents these name servers from sending the same response to the same client too frequently

RRL is actually a solution to the *use* of DNS servers as amplifiers in DDoS attacks; unfortunately, it doesn't really help when your DNS server is targeted in an attack. Since the attack on Dyn was launched from IoT devices, RRL probably wouldn't have helped.

(*Source:* Used with permission from Cricket Liu of Infoblox Inc.)

The bottom line: DNS services are evolving rapidly, and it is in our best interest to make sure that our IT groups follow the evolutionary curve closely, instead of waiting for an attack to justify change.

References

1. "Unified Extensible Firmware Interface." (2017). en.wikipedia.org. Accessed December 26, 2017, from https://en.wikipedia.org/wiki/Unified_Extensible_Firmware_Interface
2. Varia, J. and Mathew, S. (2014, January). Overview of Amazon Web Services. media.amazonwebservices.com. Accessed December 26, 2017, from https://media.amazonwebservices.com/AWS_Overview.pdf
3. "Flexnet Publisher." (2017). en.wikipedia.org. Accessed December 26, 2017, from https://en.wikipedia.org/wiki/FlexNet_Publisher
4. "Dyn Statement on 10/21/2016 DDoS Attack." (2017). dyn.com/blog. Accessed December 26, 2017, from https://dyn.com/blog/dyn-statement-on-10212016-ddos-attack/

Chapter 14

Hybrid Cloud

Hybrid Clouds Mix Components of Private and Public Clouds

The bottom line difference between public and private clouds comes down to that extra layer on the public cloud to handle the inherent multi-tenancy attributes that allow public cloud vendors to leverage their cloud infrastructure investments into profit. What the IT world is coming to realize is that multi-tenancy attributes also make cost accounting for cost sharing across departments easier. So although a private cloud might have the application programming interfaces (APIs) for billing, the backend billing system is not normally part of the system. What a billing interface does provide is a way to more fairly allocate shared costs based upon real usage (CPU, Disk, RAM, I/O, etc.) instead of guesstimated numbers.

What moving to a private cloud infrastructure really does is create a structure and methods for a higher level of end-user self-service while still meeting the control requirements of the IT organization, which must maintain security and accountability. The downside to fulfilling the end-user wish list is the level of planning involved. Providing an easy way for workgroups to stand up a customer relationship management (CRM) system for a project means that IT groups need to quantify everything that goes into that CRM and think about the variability and requirements of the CRM or any other system.

The templates, automation, and other tools available with hybrid clouds allow IT staff to be more hands off. In doing so, they delegate much more responsibility to the department level. The ability to delegate provisioning downwards really means that IT needs to shift their resources to make the templates more bulletproof and do more of the systems validation up front, rather than during the rollout process. With software-defined networking (SDN) on the horizon, the hybridization of the cloud is a great opportunity to start re-architecting your network by taking advantage of the SDN features being offered for private clouds. The SDN interface, in one form or another, will serve as the link between private clouds and on-premises systems to the pubic cloud, whether it is for load balancing or as a DMZ-like system, as you make your way to federation.

A Hybrid Cloud Will Often Feature Mostly Private Features with Some Public Functions Added

The feature leading commercial customers in their charge to public cloud is load balancing or surge capacity. The IT industry is currently unwilling to commit fully to public clouds, especially with the US Government waffling on corporate rights to privacy in a shared resource such as a public cloud. A good example of why businesses worry is the March 12, 2009, seizure of disks and servers at Crydon Technology's colocation facility in Texas. This action unintentionally shutdown Liquid Motors Corporation, which had its servers housed there. Liquid Motors certainly wasn't the target, but as a result of the seizure, they defaulted on contracts with their customers. This example sits along with cases like that surrounding the seizure of Kim DotCom's Megaupload Ltd., as well as other cases around the world in which innocent corporations got caught up in sweeping seizures from court orders seeking evidence about other tenants of the cloud facility.

The executive suites in America have been frightened out of their minds by sweeping seizures and horror stories about losing the right to privacy in the public cloud. This also explains why giants like Microsoft and Amazon are vigorously fighting the legislation enabling these actions. What the authors have heard from business executives is that they want to maintain control over their data, and while the cloud sounds great, they don't want to be put into the same situation as Liquid Motors. The American executive suite doesn't seem willing to dive into public clouds, but they want the flexibility and features of a cloud architecture, and private clouds seem to be OK since the data and systems stay in their control.

The reality is that surge capability is where corporate finance staff seem willing to authorize dipping corporate toes into the public cloud pool. No bean counter wants to let the IT group spend money on extra infrastructure for possible surge traffic, but they also don't want to walk away from the potential sales and revenue that such a surge could represent. Here is where a hybrid cloud makes a huge amount of sense, even for the change-averse executive suite.

The idea of keeping critical corporate data in a private cloud, with copies ready to handle surges in the public cloud, just isn't as scary. The investment is low and so is the risk, while still providing a way to pluck all the low-hanging fruit of a traffic surge. Then, best of all, when the surge dies off, you can shut down those public cloud images and lower your costs to almost nothing—or at least down to a lot less than maintaining hardware in your own data center.

The emerging technology everyone should keep their eye on is SDN and how this cloudy network technology is going to bridge the gap between public and private clouds—literally erasing boundaries—while, in our opinion, making it easier to implement much more aggressive protection through zones and compartmentalization, with deep packet inspection (DPI) between them.

The important part of this supposition is that SDN allows you to hide the middle of your network. Not truly hide, but rather create an abstraction layer that provides an increased set of tools for network admins to extend the reach of their network and allows them to extend departmental/organizational boundaries beyond physical locations. This middle of your network doesn't necessarily need to conform to physical boundaries, and some implementations provide for WAN routing such as Border Gateway Protocol (BGP) to link portions of your SDN cloud across encrypted links to public clouds and/or to private hosted clouds. The huge carrot for IT managers is that with SDN, your network acts more like a single HUGE switch, instead of a collection of smaller ones. The ability to sweep a policy change for your entire enterprise from a single interface is a truly tempting feature for your typically overworked networks team.

Other Hybrid Clouds Will Be Mostly Private, with Public Components Available for Dynamic Capacity Adjustment

The first dynamic capacity hybrid that we heard about publically was from Microsoft and was part of the Windows® Server® 2012 R2 rollout by the Microsoft® Server and Tools Division. The announcement demonstrated how the new Microsoft Azure® Services for Windows Server 2012 R2 could dynamically move virtual machine collections between the private data center and the Azure public cloud—all based upon a set of user-definable business rules.

Previously, major users could use tools, such as those from F5 Networks, Inc. and Coyote Networking, Inc., to globally balance traffic to a site and based upon load-balancing rules, utilize VMware® APIs to control virtual servers, either in public or private data centers. The Interop™ show took this a bit further and demonstrated how globally load-balanced virtual servers could be used to shift load based upon client location, but also would shift load to the show venue during the show and back once the show was finished.

Key Security Issue for Hybrid Cloud Is the Point at Which Data Transitions from Private to Public Cloud and Back (the Authentication Weakness)

The key issue with the transition is the transition itself. For most, the pain point of public cloud systems is that they are, for the most part, configured as an island, and in this day and age that island is surrounded by shark-infested waters. Do you build a three-lane bridge to that island in the form of a site-to-site VPN or SDN for the whole company or do you force your users to have individual encrypted links over technology such as SSL-VPNs or even simply SSL-based web portals? What does the future hold for getting access to our islands of computing? With changes like those announced by Level 3 Communications, LLC to provide SDN across the WAN, the marketplace is certainly making its opinions known about SDN adoption.

The link technology you choose isn't even close to being cut and dry, but rather more about how you do business. For that matter, those linkages could be a mix of different technologies and a migration plan to adopt emerging technologies as certain milestones are reached in their maturity.

Going back in time just a bit, forcing your users to do two or more logins to do their job was fine in the old days, but today layering on completely separate sets of login credentials is a fast way to kick off a user revolt. The world of single sign-on (SSO) is here, and if you're not using it, you should at least be taking a VERY hard look at it. Having a single ring to unite them all (sorry for the Tolkien reference) also means that a single stolen password will throw open the barbicans, exposing your whole kingdom. SSO is moving in a direction toward a single sign-on AND some sort of multifactor authentication system—something you know, and something you have. The HUGE advantage of SSO revolves around quickly revoking credentials if they're compromised, and with a single authentication source, a single change also means fewer forgotten logins to leave systems vulnerable, and, most importantly, a single place to change a lost or stolen password.

The chink in this armor is that any SSO system works best with a single authentication authority. This is all fine if you're a completely Microsoft Active Directory® shop, but what happens if you merge with a Mac® shop or a Linux® shop? With corporate consolidation running rampant, multiple authentication authorities have become all too common, and the question remains, Do you merge, split, or share the authority?

Let's look at the strengths and weaknesses of the major existing technologies to link the public and private worlds. What are the issues for each of these building block technologies for the cloud, both public and private?

SDN: Software-defined networking systems are inherently using a server where SDN devices get configuration and authentication that looks suspiciously like a URL. Considering that many of these servers have, at their foundation, either Microsoft's Internet Information Services (IIS) or an open source web application server, the authentication infrastructure isn't going to be that different from what folks are already used to. What it does mean is a heavier reliance on certificates and the ability to use wildcard certifications for this system seems to be unevenly implemented. Please note that most of the vendor demos do NOT touch the public Internet for this very reason. This is one technology that could very well benefit from another emerging technology, and that's DNS

DANE,[1] where you can embed public keys into a DNS record instead of paying for yet more certificate charges for every switch in your network. (Not all systems support wildcard certificates.) Here, the key is to be able to trust your DNS server(s) and, to that end, the emerging technology is fully dependent upon worldwide organizational implementation of secure DNS (aka DNSsec[2]). What this abstraction layer does require is attention to the security, especially at the SDN Server[3] where intrusions could potentially collapse the network or provide ways for introduction of man-in-the-middle attacks.

- **Pro:** Users have fewer barriers to get to resources, and admin can now meet user requirements in ways only dreamed of before.
- **Pro:** Being able to more easily tie compartmentalization all the way up to the application layer can also mean dramatically better security.
- **Con:** Once someone is on that network with SSO credentials, potential damage can cross geographical boundaries more easily.
- **Con:** It's a brave new world full of training and forklift upgrades.

VPN: Virtual Private Networks have been the bread and butter of remote access for the better part of two decades—Internet Protocol Security (IPsec) for site-to-site and Secure Sockets Layer VPN (SSL-VPN) for single-user access. But both still require an authentication source, especially if you want to leverage SSO so that you don't drive your user community crazy. Although VPN technology has incrementally become much easier to implement, there still exists some pretty big variations in how they're set up, and most importantly, maintained. IPsec seems to have finally reached a point at which one can expect different vendors to comply with the standards closely enough that even consumer routers can connect to the enterprise. At issue is, Should you? We're all pretty much in agreement that only having outward-facing defenses is at best naïve, and your firewall needs to at least be looking both ways. We would suggest that a VPN from a home router to the enterprise or cloud should NOT be considered a trusted link, but rather just another zone for the firewall IDS/IPS to look at.

- **Pro:** It's tried and true, and it works.
- **Pro:** IPsec VPNs are nearly universally compatible now.

- **Con:** SSL-VPNs are still vendor specific.
- **Con:** Vendors always have their little glitches, which means that the IPsec proposals aren't always compatible, and, sometimes, you end up settling for the least common encryption standards that work.

VDI Gateways: The whole concept of the virtual desktop infrastructure has enamored the executive suite since the acronym was coined. However, too often they misinterpret the sales pitch as just a way to save on desktop licenses. The reality is that VDI is more like the old mainframe model, where all your user sessions are run in the data center, and, most importantly, updates and changes can happen in a single location instead of through costly in-person visits by IT staff. First and foremost, VDI is more like a constellation of closely orbiting pieces that all have to have varying levels of trust interrelations to make it all look seamless. In providing access to a collection of virtual desktops, you also provide a way to remotely access computing horsepower inside the data center. Not bad. Just be cautious, because a virtual desktop that doesn't refresh from a template at each logoff also means that malware could potentially get a foothold onto a trusted workstation the same as a trusted workstation in an office space. At the time of writing, every single VDI solution we've touched is incredibly complex, and even with the guided installations and/or wizards, current VDI solutions with an encrypted gateway are a non-trivial system to implement. The moving parts involved with setting up and configuring a VDI gateway with SSO into virtual desktops is still a process that needs to be taken slowly, and with copious notes. There are enough moving parts that there are lots of places where you can, out of frustration, just use the administrator as a proxy, but you really should have used a tailor-made user who has just enough permissions to do their job. All the big players have some pretty decent how-to guides but have rarely paid much attention to clearly defining the roles and needs of proxy users—users who do credential look ups, power up/down machines, and have many other critical functions. (Too often the vendors make the assumption that your staff has intimate knowledge of their system, and even things like help icons refer back to proprietary terminology, which all too often leads IT staff to guess what the install script is really asking for.) The whirlwind of moving parts rise as you start looking at stepping into trust relationships of multiple authentication/directory systems for federation.

- **Pro:** Updates and upgrades to workstations are fairly easy.
- **Pro:** Now you can run complex heavy apps such as 3D-CAD on an iPad®.
- **Con:** Licensing is as complex at the system, and everyone wants their compensation in fees.
- **Con:** It isn't less expensive than stand-alone workstations; cost savings really only appear if you calculate in HR costs for workstation maintenance.

SaaS: Of all the modern virtual offerings, Software as a Service is by far the closest to the old mainframe model and includes the likes of Google[4] and Sales Force[5] in its membership. Here the idea is that the abstraction is literally up at the application layer,[6] where tools such as database, authentication, translation services, messaging, and custom apps run as services and are called by end-user interfaces. The idea here is that because your software runs on top of the SaaS abstraction layer, the cloud vendor can more easily move it around to dynamically meet load demands, provide maintenance windows, and upgrade. As for a mainframe, the developer only really has to care about the API calls and can disregard the underlying platform. The downside is that you are tied to only the tools provided by the cloud platform, and customization is limited to the coding tools provided. The upside is that SaaS can nearly divorce your IT department from data center resources for those applications.

In what has to be a marketing move, in 2014 Google announced that their entire workforce will be abandoning dedicated workstations and moving to SaaS. With Google office automation apps being what they are, the move to Chromebooks™, Chromeboxes™, and the like has become a very real possibility. What Google's SaaS strategy could do is provide a level of user and enterprise application integration that only currently exists between the Microsoft Office® suite and its world of enterprise servers. Interestingly enough, the high cost of licensing and the low cost of the Google application suite has created a massive shift to Chromebooks by K–12 education in America. To get user status inside of a document and escalate the communication from text, to voice, to video the following comprises a comparison of the various processes involved.

Microsoft's Office Suite: The Microsoft Office suite has the ability to link to Microsoft Exchange Server® and Lync®. To more easily share documents, you would more than likely also implement SharePoint®. This constellation for medium-size organizations would translate to at least four virtual servers or Office 365® Business Premium accounts for your users.

Google: Previous Google Apps™ will do the job, but in order to make a better comparison, the deployed solution would probably be more like Google Enterprise since that is where you can actually park your domain with Google and group your users in a way more similar to the Microsoft services. You do lose some granularity in organization-wide control since Google Admin doesn't have as many control knobs as Microsoft's WMI and Active Directory.

- **Pro:** No more data center, at least for those apps.
- **Pro:** Licensing is nearly all encompassing.
- **Con:** Rigid development requirements, and you don't always have a choice on development tools and/or languages.
- **Con:** You can't always link your organizational authentication to the SaaS environment; sometimes you can only settle for periodic synchronization.

Interestingly enough, both of these SaaS platforms are no longer just purely SaaS but also combine Platform as a Service (PaaS) with virtual desktops. At the time of writing, the level of integration isn't quite what you would expect from an enterprise VDI solution, but with market demands being what they are, we're pretty sure that cloud-based VDI isn't too far away.

Depending on Type and Security of Functions, If a Private Cloud Expands into Public Infrastructure Because of Capacity, Requirements May Be Critical

Private Cloud Means You're Paying for 100% of Your Capacity 100% of the Time

A private cloud isn't much different from a virtualized data center; you're just adding some cool new abstraction layers to make it more flexible.

However, like any data center on earth, you're paying for it whether you're using it or not. So if you design surge capacity into a private cloud, it means, at the very least, that contingency equipment and software is costing you money just to sit there. It also means that if you expect those contingency systems to work, you'll have to fire them up once in a while to do updates, maintenance, and synchronization.

Surge Capacity and the Capacity Rubber Band

What we'd like to see as a capability is currently only really available from high-end load-balancing systems. The scenario is that demand has spiked on the e-commerce site and we'd like to collapse non-critical systems to shift resources to accommodate an oversubscribed environment for a short time so that we can give up those resources to handle the surge. Although we've seen it done in straight virtualized environments, the emerging private cloud systems can keep associated resources together as a package. This way, if you're slowing down something like CRM, it slows down the entire collection of servers that make up CRM, instead of needing to create business rules for each separate virtual machine. We keep seeing hints of this kind of surge action set being hinted at by several vendors, but at time of writing, all the major players seem to need a third party involved in order to implement the business rules for handling surge.

Did You Pre-Plan the Trust Relationships and Prepare to Secure the Surge?

So perhaps you want to get onto the public cloud surge bandwagon? Here, the question is whether your staff members have done any sort of simulations or synthetic traffic systems to make sure surges are handled correctly. Some of the most common mistakes happen when everyone is determined to save a penny, and they neglect to do the proper wording to make sure that the cloud provider can actually honor that service-level agreement (SLA). We're still wondering why testing in the enterprise has nearly disappeared, but it has, and a prominent example is how badly Healthcare.gov was handled as it went online. We should point out that just because the cloud provider brags about a 10gig feed into their facility, doesn't mean they provide a full 10gig to the server. There are lots of potential bandwidth bottlenecks all along the network spider web, up to and including the fact that the server itself needs some fairly significant computing resources into order to even come close to moving that much data. Since most cloud vendors aren't going to tell you exactly what kind of server you're systems live on, it's probably best to try to run some synthetic traffic to help identify where your weak link is. One surprise we recently ran into was when we found out that one vendor only provisioned a gigabit virtual switch in the normal service plans, and you'd have to pay for the premium service before you could take advantage of the 10gig vSwitch. We also discovered that there were extra charges for every vSwitch, and even more to bring those vSwitches to the real world with IP charges. So, to keep the project under budget we compromised, thinking it would be fine. However, we ran some synthetic traffic using WebLOAD™7 and quickly found out that our bottleneck was with the conversation between the application server and the backend SQL server. It looked fine, but this particular error didn't get revealed until we actually ramped up the load with synthetic user traffic. There are many synthetic user load-testing systems on the market with varying amounts of capabilities—from free open source to sophisticated commercial systems.

References

1. "DNS-Based Authentication of Named Entities." (2017). en.wikipedia.org. Accessed December 26, 2017, from https://en.wikipedia.org/wiki/DNS_based_Authentication_of_Named_Entities
2. "Domain Name System Security Extensions." (2017). en.wikipedia.org. Accessed December 26, 2017, from https://en.wikipedia.org/wiki/Domain_Name_System_Security_Extensions
3. Weinberg, N. (2017). "Is SDN Your Next Security Nightmare?" Network World. Accessed December 26, 2017, from https://www.networkworld.com/article/2174811/lan-wan/is-sdn-your-next-security-nightmare-.html
4. "Google Cloud Computing, Hosting Services & APIs." (2017). Google Cloud Platform. Accessed December 26, 2017, from https://cloud.google.com/
5. "What Is Software as a Service (Saas)?" (2017). salesforce.com. Accessed December 26, 2017, from https://www.salesforce.com/saas/
6. "OSI Model." (2017). en.wikipedia.org. Accessed December 26, 2017, from https://en.wikipedia.org/wiki/OSI_model
7. WebLOAD and License Network. (2014). "Webload." sourceforge.net. Accessed December 26, 2017, from https://sourceforge.net/projects/webload/

Chapter 15

Working with Your Cloud Provider

We don't really need to spell out how contracts work, other than to point out that a service-level agreement (SLA) is in reality the memorandum of understanding between the customer and the service provider. It isn't a mutual suicide pact, where one party or the other is going to extend themselves into destructive measures just to be honorable in fulfilling the agreement to the letter. Reason has to prevail, and sometimes one party or the other may need to violate the agreement in order to stay in business. Although it may be VERY tempting to simply sign the paperwork, it really is in your best interest to first take it back to your office and sit in a quiet corner with a highlighter. Look at the SLA in terms of before, during, and after to determine what happens if some sort of significant event occurs. You also need to be realistic about looking for your legal recourse in the document as to what your exposure will be if, for some unknown reason, you find yourself needing to walk away. We like to use the old *who*, *what*, *where*, *when*, and *how* as a litmus test for contracts in general, and SLAs specifically.

Security Service-Level Agreements

They say that the "devil is in the details," and the boilerplate of the SLA is one of those documents that spell out the responsibilities of both parties. It is NOT a one-way agreement, and the customer is typically expected to exercise reasonable due diligence in protecting their proprietary information, security, and maintenance. We typically like to suggest that you keep in mind that you're a guest in someone else's facility, but because you're paying rent, you can expect certain privileges. Notice we're calling them privileges, not rights! The service provider, in turn, is expected to provide a defined level of uptime, maintenance times, sometimes speeds, levels of physical and cyber security, upgrades, personnel security measures, and, of course, things like power and cooling. Although certainly not an exhaustive list, the terms of the SLA vary widely, and many times the provider will have varying service levels depending upon commitment levels (aka cost) and premiums (add-on packages).

Considering our involvement with many different professionals, here are two slightly different opinions on SLAs:

Joel Snyder of Network Computing and Opus1 Consulting shared the following view on SLAs:

SLAs are un-negotiable because the provider doesn't have the time, energy, or interest in negotiating them. If you think about it from a provider point of view (and I've been on both sides of the fence, as a provider, and as a consumer of providers), they have a service that they engineer and monitor and that's about it. You can request all sorts of performance guarantees, but they won't be doing anything differently from your point of view than for any other customer (unless you actually buy a different service, like multi-home fiber/ SHARP). In other words, if you say "I want 99.99 uptime" and the default they sell is 99.97, then it's not like they're going to do anything different for you—what would they do differently?

At the same time, measuring SLA compliance is difficult if not impossible. Are we talking uptime? Well, then what are all the components in the path? If the loop provider cuts the loop, does that break the SLA? As you get out of simplistic services such as point-to-point copper, the SLA gets very complicated to measure and define. When you're talking about application availability over the Internet, it's essentially impossible to come up with a meaningful definition (with emphasis on "meaningful").

And, let's suppose you negotiate an SLA and the provider doesn't meet it. So what? How does this help your business? It's your responsibility to engineer for a reliable service that meets your needs, and you can't simply dump that on someone else and assume that it will magically solve the problem.

Now, SLAs internal to a company, department-to-department, I have seen work pretty well. In that case, they actually lay out expectations and help both sides understand what is expected. This is clearly true in situations where the S service being provided is not one that naturally is up 24x7; things like Email hosting are a good example, where we all know that some maintenance is required, but we need to agree ahead of time when and how much is allowed.

I'd close by noting that Opus One, my company, has paid, literally, millions of dollars to service providers; we have collected hundreds of dollars in SLA penalties. After 20+ years buying these services, I can't imagine how the SLA would have changed our experience with anyone.

That time is better spent selecting the right service provider, doing due diligence, and making sure that you and they understand what you need—rather than trying to stick it in a document which is only of interest to the legal department.

Karl Auerbach's view as both the inventor of IPTV, a lawyer, and an at-large board member of ICANN, when asked about negotiating an SLA:

We asked Karl: A service-level agreement is a contract, but isn't it still an agreement that should be negotiable?

Karl Auerbach's answer: Of course it should be negotiable—and you can leave the door open for periodic review and adjustment (by mutual agreement, of course.) That's why it is important go get your own legal counsel involved from the outset—they know, or should know, how to create agreements with the desired degree of rigidity and flexibility.

When writing contracts, it's often a good idea to try to think of everything that could possibly go wrong, and what to do about it, and what to do about it if the other side can't, or won't do what it needs to do. And then assume that you've covered only a part of all the bad things that can happen.

Remember, the other guy might look at the contract as the price he needs to pay to walk away and leaving you hanging. The legal process generally tries to turn contract failures into money payments, so if you absolutely need something done no matter what the cost, you need to build in contractual mechanisms that turn into money—for example, failures of the other guy to react should be measured in some sort of liquidated damages per unit of time of the failure. (Those liquidated damages need to have some ties to reality—terms like a billion $ per hour will probably not fly should push come to shove. The legal system tends to frown deeply on contract provisions that are clearly punitive and not reflective of some actually incurred harm.)

When specifying performance metrics, i.e., the service level, be as quantitative and objective as you can—qualitative and subjective measures are an invitation to dispute. So set up real metrics that both sides can see and use—and it's useful to go through some tests to make sure that both sides see the same numbers. And make sure that those numbers are recorded as part of your and their routine practice and not only when things go awry.

And when I say quantitative, I mean that you specify the data sources and formulas. For example, what does 99.999% uptime mean? That you can ping a box and that over a period of 7 days (measured by a GMT time base) that every ping you send (you need to specify the sending pattern) you get exactly one proper response, except for one? Or does that 99.999% mean something at a higher level than mere pings—for example, if you are offering database services do you mean that 99.999% of the SQL queries are properly handled within a time window of X milliseconds for each query?

Even a service outage of the first full year still meets a 99.999% threshold if the service company can claim that for the next 99,999 years that they will be perfect.

But don't use the contract only as an after-the-fact weapon should things go wrong. Rather build into the contract some specific procedures to be followed at the first signs of trouble—it's better to quickly solve a problem than to fight over the wreckage later. And it's always useful to occasionally exercise those procedures—like give a call to the other guy's NOC on occasion to make sure that the phone number still works. If you have a really big dependency, go visit every now and then so that you know some faces, and they know yours; that'll make it a lot easier to work through an ongoing problem without anyone flying off the handle and making things worse.

And always have a Plan B that you can use if the other guy simply vanishes and leaves you with no service, with the data on their boxes unavailable to you, and nobody to talk to to get anything done.

And remember, in these days of tough financial times, the other guy might be forced to do things that do not make you happy—so make sure that the ownership of data and code is clearly specified: You hardly want your data to be tied up inside some bankruptcy proceeding with some creditor of the service company claiming that they own your data.

And be sure of the physical jurisdictions involved. I was surprised with Amazon S3 when I retrieved some files and discovered that they were coming back to me from Italy!

There's other stuff as well—for example, if you are doing anything involving trade secrets you need to do the right thing to protect your interests. A large local university backed away from some Google-based services because they realized that they could lose their patent rights because they were arguably disclosing unfiled ideas to a third party, Google. And if you have medical data or stuff that has privacy import, you must make the service company responsible in accord with whatever those particular laws say.

Writing a good SLA takes both tech smarts and legal smarts—it's not the kind of thing that can be written by techies and thrown over the wall to the legal group.

A. Define Scope of Agreement (Which Parts of IT Are Covered)

It's our opinion that scope is the single most important piece of any agreement. Just what are you agreeing to and how are you defining those details? If you can't quickly list the expectations, then perhaps you need to work on the SLA a bit more. The sad fact is that too much trust is put in MBAs and lawyers and not enough in common sense. Not that we don't need both, but a common ground has to be met for agreements to be workable and not a mutual corporate suicide pact. Let's put it into perspective: You're looking at using the cloud for some fairly major pieces of your organization or you would not be reading this book. So it is in everyone's best interest to sit down with your legal representative and make sure you have a meeting of minds on just what you need versus what you want.

B. Define Security

The Internet world is no longer the kind, gentle place that academics built decades ago, and there are those that would like nothing better than to tear down your work just to make a name for themselves. Among them are, of course, your competitors who would love a bigger piece of the market and would like nothing better than to have the market to themselves. The bottom line is that the world is changing, and although it's quite cynical to say, "There are no such things as friends when it comes to money," especially when you're getting ready to pay out a fairly decent amount of money over a fairly long period of time. So let's make sure we're defining what you can expect in terms of security and that you have some options for defense in depth instead of only outward-looking castle walls. The barbarians aren't at the gate; they're mixing with the villagers and are wolves in sheep's clothing. If your security team is moving towards zoning and omnidirectional security for your home office, why not demand the same thing for your foray into the cloud?

So here's the rub: Inserting network taps and zoned defense firewalls into a physical network isn't too tough, and hopefully your home office already has something to detect the barbarians mixing with the villagers. However, the cloud is a slightly different castle to defend, and its flexibility is truly a double-edged sword.

There are certainly defense tools available for physical networks, and many of those same vendors are introducing tools that also leverage their experience for the virtual world. Depending upon who your monitoring partner is, they may recommend virtual taps to provide insight on the virtual switch traffic for external analysis tools; or your monitoring partner may use virtualized analysis tools peering directly onto the virtual switches through some sort of promiscuous interface on the vSwitch. In the virtual/cloudy world, you may no longer have little Johnny plugging his infected laptop into his dad's datajack behind your firewalls, but instead you may have a departmental customer relationshipment management (CRM) accidentally do an infected update that no one had time to test first.

C. Define Performance to Be Met

There was a time when corporate IT would fight over infrastructure testing professionals, but alas those days seem to have disappeared. All too often, the decision makers are taking the word of the sales team and buying products that their IT teams haven't tested first. Why is this? Very few people will buy a car based upon just a sales brochure. They would at least look at a car magazine, check with Consumer Reports, Inc., or take a test drive. The same should be applied to a cloud service provider. What kind of performance do you need: now, tomorrow, and next month? Are you hoping for or expecting a surge from some sort of public exposure? Do you need to think about global load balancing and, if so, what regions will your customers come from? If you can't answer these kinds of questions, how can you possibly expect a SLA to meet your needs?

D. Define Remediation, Relief, and Penalties If Performance Targets Are Not Met

Just how big an impact do outages, breaches, or data loss make on how you do business? Are these events your responsibility, the providers, or a little of both? Key to this discussion is the question of whether you're having unreasonable expectations that will force your provider to just pay you off. In this case, we're huge fans of the hybrid cloud, since this means you can keep duplicates of key data sets inside the castle and perhaps not depend upon the provider for everything. Here we're also VERY fond of Karl Auerbach's statement, as quoted previously:

> But don't use the contract only as an after-the-fact weapon should things go wrong. Rather build into the contract some specific procedures to be followed at the first signs of trouble—it's better to quickly solve a problem than to fight over the wreckage later. And it's always useful to occasionally exercise those procedures—like give a call to the other guy's NOC on occasion to make sure that the phone number still works. If you have a really big dependency, go visit every now and then so that you know some faces, and they know yours; that'll make it a lot easier to work through an ongoing problem without anyone flying off the handle and making things worse.

We're of the opinion that once you've come to an agreement on the terms of an SLA, those terms also need to be created so that they can be confirmed BEFORE an emergency.

Trust Relationships with the Provider

Security comes in many forms, and we'd like to point out that it would be best to take a good hard look beyond cyber access, to physical access to critical systems. Many attacks are only possible through physical access to the infrastructure, and these are why service providers tend to restrict physical access to a select few.

An important question here is, Just how is this security verified? In today's world, the industry standard has become a mix of industry standards by organizations such as the ISO (International Organization for Standardization),[1] the IEC (International Electrotechnical Commission),[2] and the PCI-DSS (Payment Card Industry Data Security Standard),[3] for credit card processing. Trust is one thing, but trusting a standards organization is yet another. In these cases, the provider has made the investment into meeting or exceeding standards agreed upon by an industry board so that you have a quantifiable level of trust in certain aspects of their operations.

Do you really need these certifications? The additional expense certainly means that the provider is going to pass these costs onto the customer. This is where you should make sure that you clearly understand your needs and wants so that you can manage the expectations for a balanced level of trust.

A. References from Existing Customers

The one thing the world keeps forgetting is that references are almost never going to be from someone who had a bad experience. So, unless your provider is willing to let you see the entire customer list and you pick at random, calling references is going to be the luck of the draw as to whether you find someone who's going to be willing to be frank about their experience. The only advice we can give here is to get a collection of references and call/email them all. So just like employment references, provider references need to be taken with a grain of salt and judged the same way. Overly enthusiastic references may have ulterior motives, whereas overly bad references may have an axe to grind. Although it might sound weird, perhaps asking someone from human resources who has experience in psychological profiling and behavioral pattern-matching for help might not be a bad idea.

B. Pilot Projects: A Brief Tutorial

One of the best pieces of advice we heard about cloud anything was that if you can't make it work in your own data center, then you don't have a prayer of it working in the cloud. Our mantra is: test, test, and then test again. And since I/O, storage, and CPU in a cloud all cost you money, we're fond of making sure it all works on a desktop or workbench first.

The other piece of sage advice we heard was that obtaining a performance benchmark in your own data center also means that you now have a way to judge your expectations for higher performance in other architectures. In this synthetic environment, you can run potentially destructive testing and, most importantly, you can also run penetration testing without having the FBI trying to break down your door. Can your app even come close to running the expected number of clients in an ideal environment? If it can't, how can you possibly expect it to support that many clients in a shared environment like a cloud?

Test, test, and then test again—both on the bench and in the cloud BEFORE you go live. Pilot projects should be designed to get broken so that you know what conditions you need to avoid in the production version. If you can't break it, then all you have is a ticking time bomb before someone out in the real world finds a way to break your project.

C. Expanding the Scope of the Relationship

Organizations certainly hope for growth, and why wouldn't you expect the same from your cloud presence? Perhaps the growth is your service provider being bought, or your organization being bought. Did you leave escape clauses? I know of one huge project that had to dump a four-month-old data center infrastructure because a company in competition with the gear they used bought them. Did you even imagine this kind of change? If you suddenly have to double or triple in size, or worse, you have to drop to half of your cloud presence, what are the ramifications? Change is said to be inevitable: Did you make allowances for it?

D. "Trust but Verify"

One of our favorite *modus operandi* in the magazine reviews game is to set up a technical support account as a regular customer and use that to judge just how good the support system for a product is. Although this sounds a bit shady, it does expose what you can expect down the line. We're both fond of spot checks to validate that there haven't been any huge changes by our providers that aren't being shared with us. What are the terms for physical spot checks? Again, there are no such things as friends when it comes to money, and verifying that support terms are being met is just a way to confirm your trust.

Assistance with Audits and Compliance

Just about every tax accountant around will tell you that they will only explain how your taxes were prepared; legal representation at an audit is up to you. Well, is your cloud provider prepared for something like a PCI audit of your credit card processing e-commerce site? Did you discuss with the provider any compliance issues involved in doing business, and is that provider prepared to partner with you? Ask a question about things such as electronic and physical logs that pertain to your compliance needs—for instance, do your auditing requirements also require criminal and financial background checks? Don't forget that the service provider is in some ways an extension of your employee force, and if you have a background check requirement for your regular employees, shouldn't you also ask the provider about these things before you surprise them with an audit?

A. Ask the Question: How Much Experience Does the Provider Have with Audits?

It's far too easy to just nod your head in a meeting when acronyms and regulatory catalog numbers get thrown out; but nothing is a substitute for experience, and this is certainly part and parcel of your partnership with your provider. Since experience is tied to the provider's human resources, a friendly call to those with experience might be something to add to your "spot checks."

B. Know the Reports: They Are Key to Success

Part of the trust relationship is having the feedback to confirm your trust, and reports run by the provider AND your IT organization should provide for both diagnostics and performance. Remember how we said test, test, and then test again? Reports are also a way to measure the health of your system(s) and should provide you with a way to measure when you've hit some important milestones for upgrades. One of our tricks is to get the same report run on our benchmark pilot project and highlight key performance factors. Keep this report as part of your training guide and part of your organizational memory. Although called many names, we call this the bus guide—what you have just in case someone falls under a bus. Better yet, make sure you cross train your staff to read those reports so that you're not wholly dependent on a single person. It's also not a bad idea to make sure you keep historical records; since some changes might not raise a red flag immediately, but over time may grow. Historical reports are similar to that old tale of how to boil a frog. If you drop a frog into boiling water it will hop out, but that same frog tossed into cold water, which is slowly heated to boiling, is going to be frog soup.

References

1. "International Organization for Standardization." (2017). en.wikipedia.org. Accessed December 26, 2017, from https://en.wikipedia.org/wiki/International_Organization_for_Standardization
2. "International Electrotechnical Commission." (2017). en.wikipedia.org. Accessed December 26, 2017, from https://en.wikipedia.org/wiki/International_Electrotechnical_Commission
3. "Payment Card Industry Data Security Standard." (2017). en.wikipedia.org. Accessed December 26, 2017, from https://en.wikipedia.org/wiki/Payment_Card_Industry_Data_Security_Standard

Chapter 16

Protecting the Perimeter

To say that 2014 was the start of some of the most breathtaking fumbles in perimeter security (Home Depot®, Target®, and, of course, Sony®) is like saying that the Great Wall of China is just like a garden fence. In all these cases, the perimeter failed in that invaders were allowed inside and never crossed a boundary that would have triggered any sort of security system. The guards were all looking outwards, while the invaders ran amok inside the castle walls. The way the world looks at network security must change from just looking outward to more of a security in-depth approach. Security now has to be approached in terms of compartmentalization similar to how the military has done it for centuries.

Military Security 101

To put this into perspective, military-style security is said to be 90% procedure, and to that end, access to secured information requires two components—clearance level and need to know. So, for example, just because someone has a top-secret clearance doesn't mean they can get to the information for project X. They require a "need to know" and are only granted access when they're "read into" a project by the project's security officer who is able to brief them on ramifications and interrelationships in the capacities and capabilities of the project. The project officer is also supposed to keep records of who has been "read into" the project. Although this sounds quite extreme, the reality is that the same types of procedures can be directly applied to the corporate world. As a result of the rules for record keeping, setting up group permissions in systems such as Active Directory® actually become a bit easier (in our opinion) since there is less guesswork about relationships between groups.

Business rules such as those *InfoWorld* magazine had can be described as need to know and classification levels. So, in the magazine's case, the reviews group wasn't even allowed to talk to the sales department, since it was a policy that no ad sales would ever influence a review outcome. Sarbanes–Oxley and the Health Insurance Portability and Accountability Act (HIPAA) have certainly set up similar business rules in that the people who create purchase requests can never be the ones that approve them, but these rules stop far short of demanding certain technologies. Consultants are said to make their money by telling you the time with your own watch. We like to say that consultants force you to stop and take an introspective view of your organization. A bit simplistic, but the idea is that modern business rules already require some separation of the business units; why not apply the same principles to your network security?

Another change that is slowly happening is where the level of trust is extended. It's still very common that a remote VPN connection is available so that someone can work from home, which is considered a trusted zone. Who's to say that little Johnny hasn't brought something nasty home on his laptop from school? Does this mean that the entire Smith family home network is infected? If, out of convenience, the Smith family home router has been configured so that John Smith Sr. can more easily work from home, has the corporate IT group also done any kind of compartmentalization of Mr. Smith's home office from the rest of his family network? We like to suggest more of a "trust but verify" attitude by making sure that Mr. Smith is at least using an enterprise grade firewall at home, and that there is some sort of multi-zone IDS/IPS system constantly testing the data flowing between headquarters and Mr. Smith's home network. In setting up a doctor's home, Brian Chee put the doctor onto one of the wired ports on the SOHO Enterprise class firewall, and the rest of the family onto the WiFi. This allowed for a separate set of IDS/IPS/firewall rules to be more easily set up and audited for the doctor's remote access, while still providing for the rest of the family to share the outbound Internet connection.

Where Does the Organizational Security Zone Stop?

We've become very fond of the keynote speech by Dan Geer at the 2014 Black Hat Conference called: "Cybersecurity as Realpolitik,"[1] where, among other things, he introduced the concept that we, as a society, need to re-examine how we treat cyber security. To paraphrase, he suggests that we need to stop thinking that a simple port-blocking firewall is good enough and suggests that these inexpensive devices are actually increasing the attack surface rather than decreasing it. The gist is that we need to increase security and to treat the residential firewall as the true edge of the network. What we really need is the ability to do deep-packet inspection[2] at the residence so that we can remove the low-hanging fruit that has become the staple of the malware bot herders.[3] Too many home routers can be exploited due to their reliance upon ancient Linux kernels, old firmware, and vulnerabilities that permit hackers to add their own software without the owners being aware—whether the intent is bitcoin mining, botnets, or implementing a man-in-the-middle attack to harvest personal information from the residence. The whole point is that it is the residential router that has actually become a weakness rather than a true security device. We're hoping that some of the new residential Internet security devices like the iGuardian by ITUS Networks (https://itusnetworks.com/ become the norm rather than the exception. We're hoping that devices that provide deep-packet inspection with a full Intrusion Detection and Prevention system based on open source software and advanced encryption CPUs (like the Cavium, Inc., security CPUs) can go a long way towards the reduction in the easy to hack residential gateways too frequently giving home owners a false sense of security. So if your residence is a workplace, then perhaps one must pay quite a bit more attention to auditing exposure potential all the way to the residence, instead of just assuming the home owner's less-expensive firewall is "good enough."

On the flip side of the coin is a group of folks that too often have the ear of IT management, and is too often the vocal minority whispering in ignorant management ears. Their position is that they've been running their machines directly on the open Internet without ill effect. To that end we say sure, if you have a fully patched operating system, and take the time and effort to check for and understand vulnerabilities on said machine, you can certainly operate safely directly on the net. We compare this to a neighborhood, where some homeowners take the effort to update their windows, doors, and locks so that they're no longer the low-hanging fruit for burglars. Are they really safe from notice of true professionals? We think not. They're just forcing the amateurs to look at the neighbor's house with weak doors, windows, and locks for a quick snatch and grab. However, if those same burglars notice a Maserati® in the garage, maybe they're willing to take the time to learn lock picking or just use a sledgehammer to break in. The point we're trying to make is that the group advocating abandonment of firewalls just because older non-zoned firewalls aren't very effective anymore, is an extremely short sighted view of how operational network security really works, especially when unlimited budgets don't exist. Until better and more effective measures become available, leveraging firewall technology such as unified threat management (UTM; combined firewall, malware detection, DPI, and IDS/IPS in a single appliance), where you can set up bidirectional threat management anytime traffic crosses a boundary—whether those boundaries are VLANs, physical interfaces, or SDN zones.

Another shot of reality is that unless you're in an environment where IT has total control of the desktop, there are always going to be priority projects that push off updates and patching. Certainly, in an academic environment, the lack of tight policies means that IT organizations have to look towards layering their security to accommodate weak links when humans forget to update or patch. The human factor is always the weak link, and it certainly makes a lot more sense to approach your security in a layered approach.

Virtual Private Networks: Have They Become the Backdoor into Your Enterprise?

The part about virtual private network (VPN) connections is that it needs to be treated just like any other unknown entity arriving on your organizational doorstep. If your security team audits the remote entity, then maybe, but if the remote location is out of oversight's reach, then maybe not. How about the myriad organizations where the regional or corporate office is the center of a hub and they've adopted a wagon wheel–like approach where store fronts connect over a public ISP back to the central data center or cloud entity. Rumor has it that in the case of a large home supply retailer, THE mistake was how their branch back office shared the same security zone as their point of sale and that they put too much trust into the VPN link back to corporate. Rumor has it that in this case, an exploit run on a back-office desktop was able to run rampant over the VPN connection and spread to other locations via the VPN. In the 2009 *InfoWorld* magazine article on UTMs, our scenario was a hub and spoke design similar to what retailers around the world use.[4] The idea was to simulate a regional headquarters connected to 2000 branch offices over a public ISP through IPsec VPNs. The testing scenario consisted of:

1. Benchmark throughput on a completely unloaded firewall to determine maximum possible throughput.
2. Do the same benchmark test, but this time with the addition of 20 simulated users at each of the 2000 branch offices.
3. Then, add the current collection of CERT attacks against the outside of the regional firewall.
4. Finally, run all the above but add in the same attacks from inside the trusted zone to simulate infected machines being brought into the enterprise.

If we were to update this scenario, and had the money for the test gear, we would have simply run the attacks over the VPN connections to see if the attacks could potentially spread themselves across zones. Best practices would seem to indicate that every single branch office would be considered a different zone, and that UTM functions would be used to examine any traffic crossing zones, even if that traffic is only exiting the enterprise. Similar tests could just as easily be run in a cloud scenario just by changing the addressing and connection scheme.

Part of any firewall-licensing scenario should include looking at just what the cost is to add a much finer-grained zone configuration across logical boundaries to support your organizational business rules. The resources are certainly there, with some truly amazing tools available for virtual switches in any major hypervisor on the market. Since software-defined networking (SDN) is really just a better way to implement VLANs (just like the Wall of China analogy; SDN isn't, but you get the idea), the need for more flexible threat management means it's probably also time to do a bit of exploring to see if what you have can be upgraded in the short term, as well as perhaps some introspective observations on how you do business to determine if you really do a need to consider a forklift upgrade. Just in case some of your networking folks try to tell you the Q-in-Q (e.g., 802.1q VLAN tag inside another 802.1q VLAN tag) is fine, keep in mind that Q-in-Q sucks up huge amounts of switch CPU, and every 802.1q tag sucks up a minimum of 32bytes of payload, which is why your networking gurus don't want a VLAN to popup in multiple locations. What SDN does is allow the processing to be handled in potentially load-balanced servers, removing a lot of CPU-intensive tasks from the switches. What this means for the security side is greater flexibility in where you can examine data flows and, in theory, fewer overloaded switches maxed out creating resource oversubscriptions that can potentially introduce new vulnerabilities.

Our big piece of advice: Don't let "sucker" get written across your forehead, think for yourself, and don't just believe what the sales team tells you. Let your staff have the time and resources to actually confirm the claims. Here's a quote from President Theodore Roosevelt:

> No man can be a good citizen unless he has a wage more than sufficient to cover the bare cost of living, and hours of labor short enough so after his day's work is done he will have time and energy to bear his share in the management of the community, to help in carrying the general load.
>
> —*Theodore Roosevelt*

(Source: http://izquotes.com/quote/262926)

So while this sounds like we've gone hugely off topic, stop and think a bit. If your management team is drunk on Kool-Aid® and pushing your staff members harder and harder to decrease costs to the point of burning them out, they'll no longer have the time or energy to increase the skills necessary to properly and securely maintain your infrastructure. Big changes such as SDN require that your staff get more than just lunchtime sales pitches. Of course, the sales team is going to tell you that product X is going to save your company huge amounts of money and time. It's also going to brush your teeth in the morning and help you lose weight. We've seen way too many installations that haven't lived up to the sales claims, not because the sales folks lied, but more because they embellished the facts, and the IT staff didn't ask the right questions.

Note: Make sure you give your staff enough time to ask the right questions.

Single Sign-On (SSO) and Multifactor Authentication (MFA)

The socially engineered hack continues to be the top way for hackers to get past your perimeter defenses, and the concept of having a single password to allow your employees into multiple services has been the holy grail of many security vendors. Now stop and think: This also means that a single password now makes multiple services vulnerable. This hidden danger is the number one reason why just about every large organization we've ever talked to that's implementing SSO is also looking at rolling out some sort of multifactor authentication (MFA) system—either at the same time or very closely following.

So just like the Post-It® note under the desk blotter, if you make the requirements too intrusive, users will find ways to bypass the complexity and create unintended consequences. The concept of something you have and something you know is an ancient one, but our modern implementations also need to take into account the human factor.

Some of the hidden dangers have been: Mobile device failures or upgrades and losing access to authentication app, using text messaging (aka SMS) but you have terrible connections for service XXX at your branch offices, that password dongle is great until the battery dies, you only register one finger and now he/she has a bandage on it, and the fun part about retina scanners is how no one is willing to stick their eye on the reader.

Let's share an example from academia to illustrate how SSO and the whole concept of a centralized authentication authority sounded great on paper, but now the bean counters have thrown a big monkey wrench into the plans. To set the stage, Lightweight Directory Access Protocol (LDAP) has long been the darling of academia because it's free. If academia only had to pay for licenses for their staff, this problem wouldn't exist, but when you add to the mix tens of thousands of students who might only be enrolled for a non-credit basket weaving class, you end up having to pay for a lot more licenses than one might have anticipated. Even that heavily discounted Client Access License (CAL) for Active Directory is too much for already tight academic budgets. Now let's take this example a little closer to the corporate home: What happens when you have an organization dependent upon temp hires, or volunteers? The bottom line is that multiple authentication sources is a lot more common than we first thought, and the number of SSO systems that can handle multiple authentication authorities is rare indeed. If they do exist, nearly all of them require some fairly complex custom coding.

We've gone a bit astray from the VPN topic, but the bottom line is that no matter how secure your remote access technology is, its weakest link is always going to be authentication. Look for those sticky notes and consider that a harbinger of a system that has become too complex to be effective.

Virtual Applications: Compromise for BYOD

We love to compare the whole concept of virtual desktop infrastructure (VDI) to that of the wheel coming back around to the mainframe days. Some of the great security benefits behind virtual applications are:

- No thick applications on a desktop for someone to reverse engineer off a stolen laptop.
- Reduction of interactions with other applications that could potentially introduce vulnerabilities.
- Increased control over updates, with increased ability for roll backs.
- No caching of personally identifiable information (PII) or other sensitive information on the local desktop.
- Multilayered permissions, both to the virtual machine that's running the application(s) and to the personnel accessing the application.
- Remote access is no longer limited to high-speed broadband connections.
- Expensive license keys are kept internal to your organization and not out in the field where dongles can get lost/stolen.
- Potentially less-secure SQL data or other data pipes are kept internal to the data center.

Like mainframes, the key to why VDI potentially has so many security benefits all lies in the pulling back into the data center those resources that actually touch anything sensitive. What this model also does harks back to the old mainframe green screen "tubes." We didn't have to worry about letting the field service provider take the old "tubes," because nothing sensitive was on them. VDI, Software as a Service (SaaS), and, especially, virtual applications have just replaced those old "tubes" with a virtual terminal window that can exist on most modern platforms. What this flexibility has also done is open up the proverbial double-edged sword of Bring Your Own Device (BYOD).

The entire concept of Bring Your Own Device has opened up a whole new can of worms in that the IT group now has to struggle with how to provide access to organizational applications without opening up the need for labor-intensive configurations and security audits of these same devices. Let's look at the security differences between virtual desktops, virtual applications, and SaaS.

Virtual Desktop is also sometimes called managed desktop or Desktop as a Service (DaaS), but it all comes down to a full Windows® Desktop, with all the bells and whistles, which also means all the audit require- ments, permissions management, and licenses. Worth mentioning is that the Microsoft® licensing rules for virtual desktop access (VDA), in some cases, have undergone major changes, multiple times per year. At the time of this writing, Microsoft has simplified and clarified many of the terms in operating system licenses for virtual environments, but these license terms can change quickly, so it's best that you check with your Microsoft sales channel for confirmation of all critical details. We advise you to be espe- cially careful to work with your channel representative to define whether you want per seat or per user licensing and to also define whether remote access is going to be BYOD or organizationally owned and whether the organizational desktop is shared or not. These seem to be the pieces of the licensing equation that most directly affect what you end up paying.

What this whole section boils down to is that, at the moment, virtual desktops are overly complex from the licensing perspective, and Microsoft seems to be encouraging BYOD through licensing. So virtual desktop remote access isn't just a technology and security issue but also a licens- ing and a BYOD issue. Our working definition is that virtual machine management and provisioning is the piece that separates remote access from true VDI. One oddity is that although Microsoft certainly has a true VDI solution, separate divisions manage the pieces, and continuity between them is spotty. So, although you could build a true VDI solution with both virtual desktops and virtual apps combined with VM management, it would take a significant amount of work to do the integration and a high degree of skill to make it all work smoothly. To give them their due, Citrix® literally created the industry with a modified version of Microsoft Windows® Server 3.51 (aka WinFrame®) and has learned quite a few hard lessons on how tighter integration has also meant a more cohesive security story.

Software as a Service (SaaS) simply put is a trend towards organizations to migrate key applications such as customer relations into web-based access and taking advantage of the relatively secure access that secure web connections can provide. The grand master of this industry segment, the folks at Salesforce.com, Inc. have spent a lot of time and energy on building up one of the biggest SaaS offerings on earth with their customer relationship management (CRM) solution. We like to compare SaaS to the old timeshare applications on Digital Equipment Corporation's VAX series and IBM®'s CICS world of remote terminal access. The similarity is that the entire application runs on the remote mainframe/platform with remote access through a relatively simple human interface. Similar to some of the last generations of smart terminals from DEC, HP, and IBM, a web interface has limited ability for input, security, and permissions error checking. Instead, much of the error checking and data validation has to be accommodated on the hosting system. The similarity goes further in that much of the security revolves around whom you login as and where you are logging in from. There is a great amount of dependency on the assumption that your web browser isn't leaving behind PII in the form of cookies, temp files, and other such things. It has even gotten to the point at which some organizations have asked for proposals for VDI solutions just so they don't have to worry about PII being left behind by the browser.

Virtual Applications was one of those virtual technologies that appeared without a lot of fanfare when Microsoft released the ill-fated Vista® version of Windows. (Remote App was also available in Windows XP Service Pack 3, but not "baked in" until Windows Vista).[5] Even without a virtualized environment, users could "launch" an application remotely with the user interface for that application showing up on their machine. The huge advantage is being able to run applications limited to only running on premise or being able to run CPU-intensive applications from a lower power machine or tablet. Another massive advantage is being able to provide remote access to thick applications with a full set of group policies (aka security and audit restrictions) without having to pass out copies of that application for remote installation on potentially weakly secured machines. Citrix and VMware® have both extended this functionality into thin or zero clients (small purpose built computing platforms that ONLY provide remote access to desktops and/or apps) and have added in features such as biometrics and MFA to meet the needs of medical and government customers. It wasn't until Windows 8 that enough of the USB redirection functionality was implemented by Microsoft to extend this outside of the Citrix or VMware world, but even then, the USB redirection was only available once the virtual machine was running.

VDI: Will Desktops in the Cloud Give IT Back Control with BYOD Running Rampant?

We've been talking *ad nauseam* about remote access with the assumption that you're building the backend infrastructure in your own data center. However, the care and feeding of huge virtual machine farms aren't the only way to provide this type of functionality. The advantages of a virtual workstation haven't been lost on the small- to medium-size organizations that just can't afford the equipment and human resource costs inherent in this type of system. What has happened is a slow emergence of a new market that's being called Desktop as a Service (DaaS) or Managed Desktops. So, although you could easily install a workstation operating system in one of the Infrastructure as Service (IaaS) providers, what was missing was the integration of self-service provisioning and integration into some sort of directory authentication system. Another part we're only just starting to see is some sort of ability to "jail" or fence in your virtual resources or at least be able to limit the scope of how far users can browse. We think many of those questions are being answered, as Cloud ISPs are able to leverage the new tools in the hypervisors and provisioning systems. Another big key is being able to federate some sort of directory-based authentication system. The idea is to NOT duplicate your entire structure but rather only carve off a portion so as to not expose more of your internal authentication tree than you need to.

References

1. "Cybersecurity as Realpolitik by Dan Geer Presented at Black Hat USA 2014." (2017). youtube.com. Accessed December 26, 2017, from https://www.youtube.com/watch?v=nT-TGvYOBpI
2. "Comparison of Firewalls." (2017). en.wikipedia.org. Accessed December 26, 2017, from https://en.wikipedia.org/wiki/Comparison_of_firewalls
3. "Bot Herder." (2017). en.wikipedia.org. Accessed December 26, 2017, from https://en.wikipedia.org/wiki/Bot_herder
4. Chee, B. (2017). "How to Stress a UTM." *Infoworld*. Accessed December 26, 2017, from https://www.infoworld.com/article/2632394/firewall-software/how-to-stress-a-utm.html
5. "Remote Desktop Services." (2017). en.wikipedia.org. Accessed December 26, 2017, from https://en.wikipedia.org/wiki/Remote_Desktop_Services#Remote_Desktop_Connection

Chapter 17

Protecting the Contents

When your data was just kept inside your organization, how to keep it from walking out the door was relatively straightforward. However, when using a cloud, the data is already physically outside your premises, so, now, what can you do? If you're using a public cloud, make sure your agreement spells out who owns the data, especially in cases of bankruptcy.

Getting the Initial Data into the Cloud

Starting a major cloud project often means getting a fairly good size initial dataset into the cloud. If you look at the numbers, trying to transfer, for example, a 2TB customer database over a cable modem connection could potentially take days, or if you get a few errors, weeks. A very old saying in the industry is to ". . . never underestimate the bandwidth of an old station wagon full of tapes . . . ," which is to say; sometimes it's faster and cheaper to ship some storage to the provider than trying to use an online file transfer. However, what happens to the drive? Have you spelled out that the drive is to be returned, or stored securely? Has the ISP made a temporary copy someplace, and have they removed that temporary copy?

Setting Up and Running Your Cloud Apps

One must take into account just how the pieces of your system communicate with each other and who or what should be allowed to talk to whom. One of your options during the initial architecture is how you carve up your virtual networks. Let's dig into this, since we've noticed that how you connect your virtual machines through the hypervisor not only determines what vulnerabilities you expose but also has the potential to create some truly massive bottlenecks.

First and foremost, your ISP is there to make money, and they probably aren't going to be handing out freebies. As part of your service-level agreement (SLA), there is a high probability that the ISP is going to limit how many of each type of virtual network interface you're going to be allowed. It's in your best interest to obtain documentation on which and how many virtual network interfaces your subscription allows and to work with your team to allocate them accordingly. For example, hiding the SQL connection on a virtual network limited to only your servers will dramatically reduce your potential attack surface. However, if your database administrator doesn't really need a 10gig interface, you could reduce your recurring costs by using only as much speed as you actually need. Of note is that in some cases which virtual network interface you choose when provisioning your servers is how they determine how much bandwidth they'll be allowing on that virtual switch. From a security standpoint you now have a virtual switch that can be part of your control surface. Who and what can connect to that virtual switch now means you have a knob to twist before access is given, which translates to malware not being able to run a powershell script to add a subinterface that can watch all the traffic on that switch. In fact, only certain network interfaces on most virtual switches can even be put into "promiscuous mode" (which means it can see 100% of the data on the switch instead of just what is directed at it).

Where and How Are You Connecting to Your App?

If this is a publicly exposed application, then you're probably using a web interface. Perhaps you might want to consider some sort of proxy between your customers and the actual app? Having something like Apache® or a commercial proxy means you have that one extra layer of checking to prevent the outside world from getting direct access to the web or application server. (Some Unified Threat Management [UTM] firewalls also provide for both web acceleration and proxies as part of their services, with load balancing as icing on the cake.) What a proxy really does is pretend it's the web server by terminating all the web traffic, and only then will it forward that traffic to the actual web server after it's had the chance to check for malicious payloads. Another big advantage is that you tend to load your Secure Sockets Layer (SSL) certificates onto the proxy, and that way the flow from the proxy to the web server is unencrypted, which makes it easier to examine, and it also separates the encryption load from the web server. The best part about this solution is that the proxy can also serve as the bridge from the public cloud interface to the private virtual switch.

Let's look at two proxy scenarios:

Simple Web Proxy *à la* Apache proxypass: Although also available on Microsoft® Web Services, the Apache proxypass is actually part of the Apache web server and has become the odds on favorite of a very large number of IT organizations around the world. Typically, one would put the proxypass server into a firewall DMZ, and then firewall rules ONLY allow the proxypass server to pass traffic to the actual web server that has no actual access to the outside world.

Another great example for proxypass is to do redirections. Therefore, for an Internet of Things (IoT)–type application, one might set up a private Access Point Name (APN) for a fleet of cellular modems. However, you never want someone to get the direct IP address of the typically weakly secured modem. Proxypass could either redirect entire Uniform Resource Identifiers (URIs) or redirect by port numbers.

The following is an Apache proxypass example:

ProxyPass /yadayada/ http://hollywood.squares.com/sienfeld

This would take the original URL of say http://cheebert.com/yadayada and send it to the real web server at http://hollywood.squares.com/sienfeld

The advantage of this is you could have a control URL for your delivery trucks that generates, for example, a weather alert. Your web app handles the authentication, but since the cellular system ONLY allows connections from your data center IP address range, the proxy will make the weather alert appear as if it was coming from that allowed IP address range, where, in reality, the weather alert might be generated from any number of your regional offices. The downside is that it is probably occurring to you that such a function could also be used for nefarious reasons—for instance, to hide information from the authorities.

Proxy at the Firewall: The glory of unified threat management (UTM) devices is that by combining the firewall, IDS/IPS, proxy, and VPN, you get a more integrated approach to building your zones of trust and the ability to create very finely grained sets of rules between those zones. The downside is that sometimes this just doesn't scale, if the UTM device doesn't have enough horsepower. It's all too common for UTMs to have a ton of features listed on their brag sheets but not be able to maintain throughput if you start turning on all the bells and whistles. We again refer back to the *InfoWorld* magazine article[1] comparing four popular UTM firewalls. The bottom line is that only those UTM vendors that have invested in hugely powerful CPUs are able to maintain throughput under load, while still being able to inspect all the packets transitioning between the various trust zones.

Where and What Are Your Authentication Sources?

We can't count how many multisite installations have forgotten about time sync. So here's the hidden danger about directory-based authentication systems. If the clocks drift too far apart, all the major authentication systems assume that someone is attempting some sort of "replay attack" wherein a valid authentication session is recorded and played back someplace else.[2] This effect becomes magnified as you start scaling up the authentication system for things such as federation and directory copies in the cloud. To that end, a very bright man named Dave Mills[3] created a way to have clocks synchronize over the network while at the same time accounting for network latency variations. His label, "stratum," indicates how many steps the reference server is from the reference for universal time (also called Coordinated Universal Time or simply UTC).[4] (The lower the number, the more accurate the clock source.) Therefore, if you should have multiple sites all sharing a common authentication database (e.g., Active Directory®), then you should perhaps have all of your sites synchronized with something like a Symmetricom® NTP Server, or, for that matter, even a simple Raspberry Pi® with a GPS receiver, which actually makes a pretty good clock source.[5] A free alternative is to use pool. ntp.org, where volunteers add their NTP servers into a globally load-balanced pool. If you point your server clocks at pool.ntp.org, you will more than likely get different servers, but overall servers synchronized across the country or world will have their clocks close enough to not cause problems with authentication.

Note: This wonderful pool of NTP servers has had their usefulness dramatically reduced because hackers have taken advantage of NTP's inherent trust (i.e., no authentication), and NTP amplification[6] attacks have taken down untold numbers of sites. To that end, more and more people are setting up their own NTP servers with an antenna that can see the GPS satellites.

Testing Shouldn't Be an Afterthought!

Time and again, we've seen cases in which production systems have failed due to unexpected load due to draft systems not being adequately tested beforehand. So, while the public has seen failures, what hackers see is opportunity. The unfortunate side effect of overloaded systems is where security systems fail to have adequate resources to handle attacks that could be found with minimal amounts of "what if" testing. During the infamous *InfoWorld* magazine firewall test, we found that the number of attacks that succeed rise significantly as load increase that one might see in a denial of service (DoS) attack. Do your systems fail open or fail closed? This is what load testing could have revealed.

What your quality assurance team needs to consider is what kinds of traffic scenarios are anticipated and to then take those traffic levels and do a "what if" or worst-case test. Typically what happens is that some sort of benchmark process will open and simulate user input on your system while using as much of the user interface as possible. In the past, *InfoWorld* magazine has used a system from Mercury Interactive (now owned by HP[7]) consisting of two pieces: WinRunner® and LoadRunner®. The WinRunner component would be the user simulator that records performance metrics, while the LoadRunner component uses scripts created by WinRunner to "load up" the application with additional synthetic user traffic. The idea is to have WinRunner recording performance metrics and also recording success or failure of authentications and inputs. LoadRunner sheds the GUI interface in order to generate hundreds or thousands of user sessions on a relatively lightweight computer. The intent is to ramp up/down LoadRunner sessions while recording the results in WinRunner. Since the system is capable of using database or script-based synthetic user inputs, it becomes fairly easy to have those synthetic users do logins, input data, do queries, and other types of typical user interactions. The system also has randomization functions so that user inputs can't become cached in any way. (Ixia Communications of Calabassas, California, also has a very capable system[8] to do similar functions that can generate both valid and malicious traffic to the application.)

Even if you don't have the budget for a commercial load-testing system, at least consider having your web development team schedule in the development of a load-testing system if you're in the Microsoft web ecosystem. Microsoft has made available a Web Performance Test Editor as part of the Web Service Commerce Starter kit. The very basic system makes use of a SOAP[9] in order to exercise the system using **Insert Request** and **Insert Web Service Request** functions. Although simplistic, it does give your development team a tool with which to create synthetic traffic in order to predict performance over varying levels of load. Since this is more of a toolkit, the level of testing is in direct relationship to the level of imagination of your team. In this case having a healthy dose of skepticism is a useful skill to have when trying to determine if your ecommerce site is going to hold up if CNNMoney.com does a story on your new widget. If you're not a Microsoft shop, there are also Java®-based systems to do something similar.[10]

Are You Building a Draft System?

If we were to pick one feature of virtualization (and thusly clouds) that we fell in love with, it has to be the quick and easy way to create an identical duplicate of running systems that can then be used to experiment on. Having a draft system is probably one of the most important things you can do to maintain your system(s). Just having the ability to roll back quickly could potentially save you untold amounts of money and customer good will.

A draft system is better than sliced bread: You can try to break it, load test it, and, in general, make sure it really is ready for your customers. It's also your chance to keep the production available (but quiescent) for a period of time so that you can roll back, should something unforeseen happen. The draft(s) is also your golden opportunity to try out upgrades, new tools, new libraries, etc. Just being able to make an exact copy of the production systems (before you roll to the backup) means you also have a great opportunity to test against the lastest version and find where that hidden danger actually came from.

Are You Repeating Your Load and Vulnerability Testing on Each Rev?

Since we already spoke about load testing, this is how we like to try to duplicate any crashes or mishaps that tend to creep into any system. This way, you refine your test scripts to try to duplicate the mishap, which then gives you a better test script for the next production version.

Since this is a book about security, drafts are also your golden opportunity to try out tweaks in your security system(s). Does that new load script trigger the correct notices in your security system? Does that new multifactor authentication (MFA) system add too much load to maintain your expected performance metrics? Are your performance metrics matching what your marketing department is bragging about? These are all good questions and all things you want to answer without testing against your production system.

Who Has the Keys to the Kingdom?

We can't stress enough that passwords should all have an expiration date, and, if at all possible, public-facing systems should try to have the ability to auto expire passwords. We can't always have someone on top of expiration dates, so we might as well use automation to take that duty off someone's plate. Better to have someone screaming about not being able to get in, than someone who's been terminated be able to continue to have access.

Brian is a big fan of password vaults, and he uses the Splash ID system, wherein an encrypted database is stored in the cloud and allows for synchronization across multiple devices. The features you need to look for are that the database NOT be readable by anything other than the app, that it be strongly encrypted, and if someone blows the access password enough times, the system will scrub the database off the storage medium. He's also fond of the SplashID™ Key Safe, which is a key-shaped USB drive that has access software in both Mac and Windows format. This version is optimized to run directly from the USB key, and when it shuts down it scrubs any temp files left over for a theoretical zero footprint. It's being mentioned here because they've released an enterprise version that allows for compartmentalization of which passwords are shared by which group of users.

Using the SplashID Key Safe is an example of what a small- to medium-size organization could do with little effort. However, what happens when you're a field service organization with field techs that need access, but shouldn't have access after that service call?

A fairly extreme solution was used by a convention center Internet service provider that leveraged the amazingly rich scripting capability of the FreeRADIUS authentication system. Here's how it worked: When the field tech would arrive to do some sort of physical work in the convention center, they would call an operations center and read the name tag off the piece of equipment. From a menu, the call center would trigger an SNMP push to the device for a single-use login name and password. Once the system would detect a successful login, it would remove the credentials behind the tech. All the connections were made through an IPsec VPN to add a second layer of confidence so that the SNMP credentials or the one-time logins weren't shared accidentally.

To take this into the Microsoft world isn't a huge stretch, especially when Microsoft's TechNet folks have shared some amazingly complete examples in their library. The Powershell example[11] for creating users from a script can be your easier way to bulk add users, but with a bit of imagination, it could also be used to set the user attributes to expire the password at the end of the day.

Our last suggestion on passwords is very much old school and that's to NEVER do work as administrator or root. We always suggest, at the very least, to make a user part of the root or administrator group and then physically print out the password with a date and seal it in an envelope. Have someone in a position of trust store that envelope and shred the old one when a new one replaces it. This way if someone leaves under adverse conditions you aren't locked out, nor can deleting files lock you out. This isn't perfect since they can still try to change the administrator password, but it gives you that one more route to save the day.

Have You Allocated Enough Time to Bring Your Documentation Up to "As Built"?

This topic has been heard over and over again, and we're as guilty as anyone else of rarely making enough time to accomplish this most ignored "last task" for any project. We've just barely made the deadline, and the entire project team just wants to take a few days off before the next treadmill. Well, here's a suggestion that worked for one of our teams, and while I doubt it will work for everyone, it could give you ideas of your own.

The end-of-project documentation party is where we can relax a bit and enjoy our success. However, you pass a laptop around as the "hot potato," and each person reads off a major section of the original project documentation, and the group then chimes in on whether you can keep it, or starts chiming in on changes that were made. By passing the "hot potato" around, no one person is stuck typing, and everyone can get their $0.02 into the final document. Brian used to keep tabs on those contributing, and the group would do a quick poll to determine if the contribution was major or minor. Minor contributions got a tick mark by their name and major contributions got five. For every 10 tick marks, you got a drink ticket redeemable anytime that year at a social event. For the non-drinkers, 10 ticks got you a free lunch. Brian also used to pass out random extra ticks for those helping the merriment along and, in general, helping to egg the others on to dredge up those changes they might have forgotten.

Did this sound like we got a bit off topic? Well not really. Protecting your content needs to be designed into any system. Who, What, Where, When, and How should always be considered in any system, and especially when it comes to protecting the keys to the kingdom.

Who can get to the keys and under what conditions? Where are you going to allow those keys to be used? When is it appropriate to delegate, and how are you going to make sure the keys aren't abused? Make up your own definitions for the Who, What, Where, When and How. But make up something that you can use as an organization-wide quick check.

References

1. Chee, B. (2017). "Malware-Fighting Firewalls Miss the Mark." *Infoworld*. Accessed December 26, 2017, from https://www.infoworld.com/article/2632304/firewall-software/malware-fighting-firewalls-miss-the-mark.html

2. "Get IT Done: Keep Perfect Time to Avoid Active Directory Failure." (2017). *Techrepublic*. Accessed December 26, 2017, from https://www.techrepublic.com/article/get-it-done-keep-perfect-time-to-avoid-active-directory-failure/

3. "Network Time Protocol." (2017). en.wikipedia.org. Accessed December 26, 2017, from https://en.wikipedia.org/wiki/Network_Time_Protocol

4. "Coordinated Universal Time." (2017). en.wikipedia.org. Accessed December 26, 2017, from https://en.wikipedia.org/wiki/Coordinated

5. "Building a Raspberry-Pi Stratum-1 NTP Server." (2017). satsignal.eu. Accessed December 26, 2017, from http://www.satsignal.eu/ntp/Raspberry-Pi-NTP.html

6. "NTP Server Misuse and Abuse." (2017). en.wikipedia.org. Accessed December 26, 2017, from https://en.wikipedia.org/wiki/NTP_server_misuse_and_abuse

7. "Automated Testing, Unified Functional Testing, UFT | Micro Focus." (2017). software.microfocus.com. Accessed December 26, 2017, from https://software.microfocus.com/en-us/products/unified-functional-automated-testing/overview

8. "LTE WI-FI OFFLOAD TEST." (2017). ixiacom.com. Accessed December 26, 2017, from https://www.ixiacom.com/solutions/lte-wi-fi-offload-test

9. "Web Services Description Language." (2017). en.wikipedia.org. Accessed December 26, 2017, from https://en.wikipedia.org/wiki/Web_Service

10. "Apache Jmeter - Apache Jmeter™." (2017). jmeter.apache.org. Accessed December 26, 2017, from http://jmeter.apache.org/

11. "Script Active Directory User Creation Tool 1.2." (2017). Gallery.technet.microsoft.com. Accessed December 26, 2017, from https://gallery.technet.microsoft.com/scriptcenter/New-User-Creation-tool-14fa73cd

Chapter 18

Protecting the Infrastructure

Protecting the infrastructure, regardless of whether it's in your data center, a private cloud server, or a public cloud server, is really about limited access to key resources. Having management interfaces open to the public isn't a great idea. Instead, consider making sure that remote access is through a mechanism that reinforces access management with some sort of transport security. Although it may sound wasteful to run an encrypted web interface through an encrypted tunnel, what this does is provide you with another line of defense. Remember defense in depth—layers of security ensuring that if one protection mechanism should have an unknown vulnerability, you haven't opened the kingdom to attack.

Protecting the Physical Cloud Server

There is a saying in the hacker community that once you have physical access to the server, all bets are off. The reality is that console access to many servers means that a simple reboot with some easily obtainable tools can give super user access. Additionally, many servers have the default IPMI, iLO, or DRAC service process user names and password printed on a sticker affixed to the server. If you're still using the default service processor password, it means a fairly quick set of changes can open full remote console access. A common cyber warfare trick is to hide a cellular modem in the rack behind the server and connect it to an open serial port. A fast console session can now quickly redirect that same console session to the serial port, which means that your attacker can take their time attacking you from afar. It should also be pointed out that if your attacker can force a reboot on many Linux® servers into single-user mode, they can run a brute force password cracker on the console and never get locked out.

Have you ever wondered why so many ISPs have cages inside the data center? It's because the locks on most racks are super easy to pick, or all use the same keys. So what many large corporations have done is to further limit physical access to their machines with robust locks or biometrics on these cages.

Have you heard of the concept of lights out data centers? The bottom line is to set up your systems so that you never need human access and thusly never have to turn on the lights. Those same conveniences also mean that you need to consider making sure those conveniences have a similar level of security as your main system. Let's take a look at these remote management tools and talk about how to balance the ultra-convenient (and time-saving) utilities and the risks unfettered access can bring.

IP-based Keyboard Video and Mouse (IP KVM) remote console switching systems are so popular that they've been integrated into most modern enterprise-grade server systems. We've used them so that data center operations personnel can get console access to the point that even server firmware upgrades are now possible. With the advent of remote-media mounting capability, it is now commonplace to reboot a server, get into the management interface, and actually present a virtual USB stick for firmware upgrades. Although the Remote Desktop Protocol (RDP) or virtual network computing (VNC) are wonderful and cheap, what it doesn't do is give you remote access if the host operating system isn't running. This type of facility has the potential of saving huge amounts of money if you can eliminate needing to drive across town just to press a single key if the boot is stuck. Now stop and think what a malcontent could do with access to this? Perhaps it's time to consider an SSL-VPN to hide these sensitive devices behind?

Console/Terminal servers have been around forever and have been the preferred way to make 100% sure that the networking team can get into the switches and routers no matter what. To put this into perspective, we'll take you back in time to 05:30 UTC on January 25, 2003, which just happened to be right in the middle of the Interop Las Vegas trade show when the Slammer Worm hit. Like everyone else, the network ground to a halt. The difference was that Interop had a set of full-time network analyzers watching our traffic, and these analyzers were able to characterize the attack within minutes. We were able to use our out-of-band management network (aka Access Ethernet) to get into the serial console ports of our routers and switches to add in rules to protect the show from Slammer. However, if we had only had in-band management for our routers and switches, it would have been game over.

Power Distribution Units (PDUs) are simply smart power strips that can be purchased in many different flavors. A good example are the units from Server Technology (https://www.servertech.com), where you can start from their configurator page (https://www.servertech.com/products/build-your-own-pdu) and choose the type (smart, metered, etc.) then the input power and plug type, then the output types. (Delta is traditional 208-volt split phase, aka L6-30's or WYE, where the phases are separated like L21-20.) The issue here is that the smart power distribution units (PDUs) have an embedded Linux server and can be configured for HTTP, HTTPS, SSH, Telnet, or SNMP control. Additionally, you can either choose the metering of each power phase (L1, L2, L3) for the entire PDU or the metering of each individual output. While metering individual outputs might sound extreme, SNMP triggers can be set up so that you can tell when someone is "borrowing" power from a neighboring cabinet, or, better yet, you can tell if a server is beginning to have power supply issues if the power draw begins to change. An important thing to keep in mind is that controllable outlets can translate to significantly fewer visits to the colocation facility—a feature that should be kept out of the public view. Again, like the management consoles for your switches and routers, the InteropNET crew separates these sensitive features onto what we call "Access Ethernet," which is only available through a VPN for trusted personnel. As with any "stripped-down" embedded computing platform, compromises had to be made and typically have limited security features that probably should NOT be put onto a public network. Just think if someone managed to brute force access to a PDU and decided to shut you down just for fun.

OOBI aggregators are great out-of-band management aggregation portals—for example, the Avocent® DSView™ or Raritan®'s CommandCenter®. With these portals, you can group management features with remote access—that is, the admin department may only have access to PDUs on Rack#6 and only power ports 11 through 24. Additionally, the management systems could group access rights to only a group of ports for admin server 2 that include IP KVM port 4 and PDU ports 4 and 5. Therefore, each remote management user could have user profiles limiting their access, both by group and user profiles. Aggregation systems like those from Avocent and Raritan provide both profile-based access and an access portal from the public realm to the isolated management network. Depending upon the version you choose, many of these aggregators also include the ability to display environmental information for devices you have rights to. Both the Raritan and Avocent versions now include the ability to read IPMI, iDRAC, or iLO service processor information and visualize fan speeds, input and output air temperatures, external temperature, and humidity sensors and others. We've even seen some systems with the ability to monitor a magnetic door switch and trigger image captures from webcams for rack security. Most importantly, these aggregators can also aggregate SNMP feeds to help reduce the overall "noise" of some monitor feeds. The key idea here is to reduce the need for physical access to your computing facility and help make more informed decisions on your physical server infrastructure.

Service processors with IP KVMs inside them have become wildly popular, especially for blade servers. Instead of forcing you to use up an IP KVM dongle for each blade, you instead insert an IP KVM module into the chassis and uplink that feed to the master IP KVM or aggregation system. It should be noted that the IP KVM feature is rarely included by default and should be something you consider as part of the original configuration for your servers. The service processor is literally a small computer that doesn't have a power switch. As long as the server chassis has power, the service process should be live. Normally, through a web interface (or IPMI, iDRAC, or iLO remote management protocols), you can get chassis environmental information, power management, and, in some versions, an IP KVM.

Why out-of-band management? The unfortunate answer is that most management facilities were tacked on as an afterthought, and in too many cases, they have relatively weak security capabilities. We strongly recommend that you consider using some sort of authentication server and avoid using local accounts. The simple fact is that those local accounts on a multitude of management devices tend to be forgotten, and either the passwords are forgotten or they are not changed during personnel changes. Having a backdoor admin still makes sense, but not one that's used outside of emergencies. Better to have these passwords stored in someone's safe or secure filing cabinet.

Now you know why we put those management tools behind a firewall in a separate zone and why many installations implement a completely isolated management network so that you can always get to things like switch and router consoles and you don't get locked out, even if someone is doing a denial-of-service (DoS) attack against your production network. The InteropNET teams calls this bottom-of-the-rack switch "access Ethernet," which is a flat un-routed network (so that router attacks won't affect it) dedicated only to management interfaces.

Protecting the Virtual Cloud Server

Protecting Cloud Infrastructure with NetFlow
Contributed by Tom Cross, Director of Security Research at Lancope®

One of challenges posed by cloud computing is that when applications move into cloud environments, IT Security teams feel a loss of visibility into and control over the associated systems and network infrastructure. In many cases, this effect is as designed—the reason that applications are migrating into the cloud is that cloud environments offer application owners the ability to rapidly deploy.

Sometimes that speed comes from sidestepping corporate procedures, which include information security standards. This creates a critical tension. On the one hand, application owners sometimes view corporate policies as a drag on the velocity of business. On the other hand, the risk that the business faces from the compromise of critical data doesn't go away when that data moves into the cloud. In the case of public cloud infrastructure, many corporate security teams are struggling to even maintain basic awareness of what applications, workloads, and data are moving into those environments. Ideal solutions to these challenges provide IT Security with awareness at a minimal cost to velocity and flexibility.

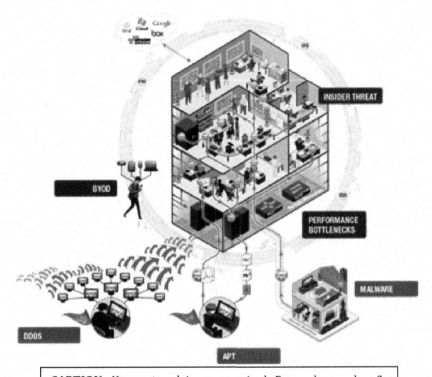

CAPTION: *Your network is compromised. Do you know where?* NetFlow collection and analysis offers a method for gaining pervasive visibility and security context.

Image: ©XPLANE 2013

Source: Reproduced with permission from Lancope®.

NetFlow is a family of standard network protocols that is spoken by a wide variety of popular network equipment. NetFlow was originally developed by Cisco Systems to collect IP traffic statistics. The NetFlow protocols carry records that are analogous to the kinds of records that would appear in a telephone bill. Each month, a phone bill provides an itemized list of all the calls that were placed, when they were placed, minutes used, rate type and the call destination. NetFlow is essentially a telephone bill for the IP network, providing similar details about each network transaction—source and destination IP addresses and port numbers, time, bytes transferred, etc. . . . These NetFlow messages can be collected from network devices and stored, providing a full audit trail of all network communications, which can be used to support a wide variety of security, network management and compliance functions.

NetFlow has become increasingly important in traditional IT infrastructure as a security tool. As the cyber security threat landscape has continued to grow in complexity, the ability to see exactly what is going on inside an enterprise network has become increasingly critical. Without being able to monitor who is doing what on the network, when and with which device, it is extremely difficult to protect today's dynamic technology environments from sophisticated online attacks such as Advanced Persistent Threats (APTs) and insider threats.

Unfortunately, conventional security solutions such as firewalls, antivirus and IDS/IPS, while still valuable, are increasingly being circumvented by determined attackers who eventually make their way into the network interior. Once they are inside, traditional tools provide little in the way of surveillance to determine what happens next. This leaves a dangerous gap in the ability of an enterprise to detect when an attacker is wreaking havoc inside the network.

However, by collecting and analyzing NetFlow and other types of flow data inherent in routers, switches, firewalls and other network infrastructure devices, organizations can regain the internal visibility needed to detect and respond to advanced attacks across large, distributed networks.

Cisco and others have developed several variants of NetFlow including IPFIX, sFlow, CFlow, J-Flow, Flexible NetFlow, etc. Because it already exists within several network infrastructure components, flow data provides a cost-effective means of filling in the security gap for today's enterprises.

The need for internal network visibility increases as enterprises embrace new technology trends including virtualization, cloud computing and bring-your-own-device (BYOD) environments. In the context of Cloud Computing, NetFlow can provide a cost effective means for IT Security teams to regain visibility into infrastructure that is becoming virtualized and moving into cloud environments. Once regained, this visibility can enable to security team to identify when new applications are being brought online, track accesses to critical data stores, and using the audit trail that NetFlow creates, investigate security incidents that involve cloud based data.

Virtualization

Virtualization delivers many benefits including lower hardware maintenance and energy costs, recovered data center floor space, higher availability, reduced disaster recovery costs, faster server deployments, maximized server capacity and increased flexibility for development and testing environments. However, when not properly monitored and managed, virtualized server environments can lead to many network performance and security concerns. For example, attackers can use hyperjacking, which involves installing a rogue hypervisor that can take complete control of a server, to launch attacks on virtual infrastructure.

Because virtual-machine-to-virtual-machine (VM2VM) communications inside a physical server cannot be monitored by traditional network and security devices, this lack of visibility complicates problem identification and resolution, potentially erasing any cost savings associated with virtual environments in the first place. Additionally, many security technologies involve too much overhead and impact to virtual servers to feasibly deploy. Unfortunately, basic access control, antivirus and virtual firewall technologies are not enough to adequately secure the virtual network.

Flow-based monitoring technologies such as Lancope®'s StealthWatch® System that include virtual monitoring capabilities can restore visibility into the virtual environment. By collecting NetFlow records for all virtual-machine-to-virtual-machine communications within the virtual environment, it is possible to get complete visibility into the transaction occurring in that environment, and record those transactions as an audit trail for investigation in the event that something goes wrong. Automated behavioral analysis of this Flow data can detect configuration problems, inefficiencies in resource allocation, and security and policy violations before any failure or degraded performance occurs.

Visibility into the virtual environment enables security teams to:

- *Manage policies within virtual environments to detect undesired connections.*
- *Baseline the virtual network to better understand normal traffic patterns.*
- *Detect and alert on the deployment of new virtual machines and applications.*
- *Identify when a virtual server is behaving in a manner inconsistent with its normal pattern, exposing potential risks to sensitive data.*
- *Provide a forensic data trail of who, what, when, where and how security events occurred.*
- *Track network events that trigger VMotion (the migration of virtual machines from one physical server to another).*
- *Avoid "VM sprawl" and limit the attack surface.*

The Private Cloud

The private cloud takes virtualization a step further by providing hosted services to employees and other privileged users behind the firewall to enable a faster, more flexible and collaborative computing environment and dramatic cost savings. Even though private cloud architecture is thought to be more secure than the public cloud since it is owned and managed by a single organization, it still introduces enhanced security risks due to its dynamic aspects, reliance on next-generation technologies and the shared nature of cloud resources (enabling one vulnerable or compromised service to more easily affect others).

As in the case of virtualization, flow-based monitoring can provide the network visibility needed to successfully transition to the cloud without sacrificing security. Administrators can use flow data to monitor for concerning behaviors such as users trying to access restricted services. In addition to pervasive network visibility, advanced, flow-based monitoring solutions like StealthWatch also deliver identity and device awareness to pinpoint exactly which users and machines are accessing the cloud infrastructure. These capabilities are particularly beneficial since one of the key drivers of cloud computing is to enable users to access corporate applications from virtually anywhere using any device they choose (a.k.a. BYOD).

The Public Cloud

Public cloud providers are becoming an increasingly attractive target for attackers because they maintaining such a large concentration of different corporate resources and data in one place. Imagine the amount of confidential information that could be obtained, for example, by just one nefarious insider at a major cloud services provider. Furthermore, public clouds provide corporate security with the lowest amount of visibility and control vis-à-vis private alternatives.

When deciding to outsource IT services to the public cloud, enterprises must perform due diligence to thoroughly evaluate the security technologies and practices being used by various providers. One way that providers can address the concerns that security teams have about moving workflows into their environments is to provide those teams with visibility into how that data is being accessed. NetFlow is an economical way to provide that visibility. NetFlow typically consumes only a very small percentage of the total bandwidth required by the traffic that it represents. Therefore, it is economical to export NetFlow from public clouds into cloud based collectors or even collection systems that are operated at the customer premise.

From the standpoint of the providers, security will become a major differentiator, and NetFlow collection and analysis can significantly help shore up security for service providers and create a competitive advantage. A highly scalable and cost-effective means of network and security monitoring, flow data can equip cloud service providers with in-depth insight across their massive networks to protect against malware, APTs, DDoS attacks and data breaches that could impact customers.

No matter which stage of cloud implementation an organization is embarking on—virtualization, building a private cloud, using a public cloud, or acting as a service provider—the collection and analysis of flow data from existing network devices can provide the visibility and security intelligence needed to avoid becoming the victim of sophisticated attacks.

About the Contributing Author

Tom Cross is Director of Security Research at Lancope where he works to improve Lancope's network anomaly detection capabilities. He has more than a decade of experience as a security researcher and thought leader. Tom was previously manager of the IBM X-Force Advanced Research team where he focused on advancing the state of the art in network intrusion prevention technologies. He is credited with discovering a number of critical security vulnerabilities in enterprise-class software and has written papers on security issues in Internet routers, securing wireless LANs, and protecting Wikipedia® from vandalism. He frequently speaks on security issues at conferences around the world.

Hyperjacking[1]: The Keys to the Kingdom

The world has certainly changed, and since we can now back up or move our entire CRM system as a virtual machine, this also means that if someone manages to get unauthorized access to the hypervisor (aka the virtualization operating system), then they can also download, modify, or move our kingdom's treasury. We tend to equate the Hypervisor control system with an extended console, and we've said before that unprotected console access is like handing the keys to the kingdom to attackers. What has changed is that in order to save money, more and more IT managers are moving to versions of Windows that no longer has a graphical user interface (GUI), which requires you to install management tools onto desktops or to manage the barebones servers from a server that does have a GUI. This, more than anything else we've talked about so far, is the reason why strong passwords changed often is so important. Being able to change user accounts across the entire enterprise becomes very important as the IT infrastructure becomes increasingly complex, and delegation also means that you can't forget to disable credentials when people leave. Just because a person only has operator credentials, doesn't mean they can't download an image of your CRM or something even more important.

As Tom Cross talked about in the previous section, being able to notice pattern changes in how your network flows is a hugely important tool. In the case of the well-known breach of the systems at Sony Corporation (https://www.washingtonpost.com/news/the-switch/wp/2014/12/18/the-sony-pictures-hack-explained/), that flow would have been many megabytes per second over a long period of time as the attackers patiently downloaded huge pieces of the Sony IT system that even included actor's personal information. Your system(s), whether in house, virtual, or cloudy, all means that being able to spot changes is hugely important, whether it's Ray's product, or something simpler, such as What'sUp® Gold with the netflow module. It all means that the ability to look into the flow patterns of your infrastructure has become more and more important as we migrate towards the cloud. It's not better or worse. It's different, and it needs a different set of tools to keep the kingdom secure.

Protecting the Network Infrastructure (Load Balancers, Accelerators, More Proxies, Managers, and More)

Just as a reminder, those appliances that handle load balancing, WAN/ SSL acceleration, and web proxies are all computers with software written by humans. If someone isn't paying attention to updates, some attacker may just stumble across your unpatched/updated device and take advantage of a vulnerability that probably got fixed while you weren't looking. Here, the thing to watch for is that a load balancer, WAN/SSL accelerator, or web proxy all have something in common. They typically have network interfaces on both the trusted and untrusted side of your perimeter defense. Making sure you don't stop at a perimeter defense and at least consider breaking up your network into zones translates to layers of defense. If a vendor makes a mistake on one of their appliances, let's hope your zone defense gives you at least one last chance to catch that attack. Also a successful attack on one of these appliances (hardware or virtual) also means the attacker now also can harvest the real addresses of your internal servers, and that compromised system can now serve as a beachhead for a more concerted attack. Worse yet, that information could be sold and that vulnerability could then be exploited by some other team of attackers or released to the world. Similar to switches and routers, if these appliances (physical) have management ports, you might consider putting them onto an isolated management network, and make sure that you know what kind of traffic to expect through them. If not a flow monitor, then at least have an idea what normal traffic levels should be, both inbound and outbound, so you know if someone is trying to transfer something out of the ordinary.

Tie a Cloud into Your Security Infrastructure

This is the part that's got a lot of people worried: What happens if you put a portion of your authentication system into the cloud? Are your ISP's hypervisors and networks secure? This is where we strongly suggest to not only depend upon the ISP's security system but to also double-check with some of your own. The promise of federation seems to be the big driving force in those organizations that would like to be able to delegate some access into your cloud infrastructure, but to limit what's actually exposed. Do you really need a complete copy of your active directory structure in the cloud, or can you strip it down to only what's really needed, to limit the potential attack surface? A directory authentication system is considered inherently more secure since you can make global changes to user accounts quickly and globally to respond to potential issues such as user migration. It also means that you have an authentication system that can also be used to secure remote access to infrastructure pieces. What we do suggest is to consider making sure you limit who and from where you can connect to that authentication system by limiting access scopes so that you can take advantage of the quick changes that a directory authentication system provides, but not expose this system to untoward advances by attackers.

References

1. "Hyperjacking." (2017). en.wikipedia.org. Accessed December 26, 2017, from https://en.wikipedia.org/wiki/Hyperjacking

Chapter 19

Tie the Cloud Using an Internal Management Framework

This is really all about making sure that you have a more coherent view of your systems regardless of whether they're on premise, in a colocation service, or in a public cloud. Documentation and a coherent view of what your systems are doing is a hugely important step into any expansion plan, cloud, or otherwise.

The Achilles' heel of security is a disconnect between developers and the security team. What may be a great development environment could very easily open up a security hole that can hide unauthorized remote access. A good example is how some popular power monitoring systems have utilized either raw TCP sockets or websockets to stream their power usage data in near real time. The attraction is how little overhead sockets in general have but at the cost of a lot of error checking. Sockets are very dependent upon the developers doing their own error checking to defend their app from abuse. The point we're trying to make here is not that sockets are bad, but rather that each technology has limitations and caveats as to how they should be used and how they need to be defended against the barbarians at the gates.

Understand the APIs Available from Your Cloud Provider

What we'd like to point out is that features have to be implemented somehow, and remote connectivity needs some sort of transport. Brian's favorite rant is how this Internet of Things (IoT) trend has spawned a huge number of players that are rushing to market without really thinking out the issues around making sure the systems don't create a whole new set of vulnerabilities. What should be considered are the basic questions of who, what, where, when, and how. Who should be able to connect to your IoT or cloud solution and from where, when, and how? Brian's IoT solutions live on a private APN that only allows connections from certain address spaces and only through encrypted connections. Emerging IoT toolkits are going further (thank the stars) and adding in certificate-based SSL/TLS connections to further reduce the possibility of some random person abusing your IoT application.

What kinds of connections play a huge part in securing any cloud or IoT application, and an emerging danger of things like raw or web socket connections, where you're literally exposing a connection socket on a network for M2M connections. Are you making sure that only certain machines can connect? Are you double-checking the input strings to make sure they're in an expected format? Are you making sure you're protecting your app from someone pushing more data than expected (aka buffer overruns)? Some of the famous vulnerabilities are where hackers are purposely pushing code as part of the payload and purposely overwriting portions of your remote code so that the device will try to run that malicious code. Adding even a single line of code to truncate inputs that are out of expected lengths can go a long way to preventing a repeat performance of some famous buffer overrun attacks.

Another famous M2M attack involves taking advantage of how many SQL server implementations have the ability to connect to other SQL servers for synchronization or even remote execution. The potential weakness is that SQL servers aren't concentrating on security, and those connections are rarely encrypted. With IPsec VPNs easy to implement, it would make a whole lot more sense to tunnel any potentially less-secure connections over a more secure connection. Although it may sound redundant, utilizing an encrypted tunnel such as IPsec makes a whole lot of sense, even if you're tunneling an already encrypted technology—for example, SSH, HTTPS, or sFTP/SCP. Just because one technology is encrypted doesn't mean someone isn't going to make a mistake in his or her implementation, and that second layer of encryption is just a bit of insurance against human error.

Diving in a bit deeper into APIs from cloud vendors, we find that cost has been driving stripped-down implementations of things such as SQL servers. Those stripped-down solutions meet a very specific need for storing relatively small amounts of data, but at the cost of additional error checking, connection checking, and a multitude of other features normally found in the full implementation. Amazon Web Services™ (AWS™) or Microsoft® Azure® implementation of an SQL database instance might be a good candidate for securing only to your cloud apps through an isolated/secure virtual network in the virtualized environment. Another thing to consider is those amazing report writers that need access to your data sources. Who is allowed to run them? Just because it's a report, doesn't mean it doesn't potentially have access to some sensitive information. Can that report writer use its default credentials to browse the user database? Reports have a tendency to be towards the end of the implementation cycle but shouldn't be short changed on the security audit step. Again, who, what, where, when, and how are all questions that need to be answered before reports are made public. We strongly believe that these five critical questions should be examined at every major step, not just at the end or beginning.

Conversations with Your Vendors: Understand How to Hook into APIs

An all too common mistake made during the planning stage is when the sales group of a cloud vendor gets overly enthusiastic about trying to fit buzz words into their sales material. The danger is when they "borrow" a term to describe a new engineering feature without really understanding that this new feature may have actually been a compromise to meet a marketing goal. A great example is how an operating system vendor had some old sales information that described a version of Remote Desktop as being encrypted, when, in reality, engineering had only implemented TLS encryption during the authentication process and hadn't quite implemented the ability to encrypt the entire data stream. The widget/control was there, but it didn't work yet. All it really needed was an update, but if you turned it on right out of the box, you'd only get authentication encryption.

Another less known API revolves around dedicated management interfaces for updating the hardware your systems are sitting on. Can your out-of-band management system be reached from the public side of the shop? When vendors go as far as labeling something as out of band, they normally mean it. That service processor on a server or router mgmt. interface weren't meant to be publicly accessible but rather should live on an isolated network specifically meant for management and security devices. The same should go for cloud systems, and if you must have remote public access, then perhaps it should be through an SSL-VPN, as a minimum. Here, the danger is that once onto a management interface for something like an Ethernet switch, it isn't that much harder to push an older version of the switch firmware onto the device and name it something new. Then, sometime later, when the device is power cycled, the switch can be configured to boot from that unauthorized version. This old version may have a known vulnerability with which the attacker could get remote access. What should be pointed out is that attackers tend to be very patient and make small steps into your systems. We liken it to collecting grains of sand, and if the attacker if patient enough, they'll eventually have their own beach.

The lesson here is that even small vulnerabilities can grow, and if you keep asking who, what, where, when, and how, maybe you can keep the attackers from establishing a beachhead into your system. Always make sure you understand your vendor's implementation of the interface and not assume it's just like the one you're already used to.

Using Appliances to Manage Cloud Security

To appliance or not to appliance, that is the question. We can't pretend to say that one is better than the other, but we can talk about where they might make sense. We should start off by saying that not every appliance is created equal, and not every security appliance design was driven by security rather than sales. A good example is those inexpensive home firewalls that really don't even deserve that name. Too many are based upon ancient versions of Linux® that have brought along a multitude of vulnerabilities as baggage. In the 2014 keynote speech by Dan Geer at the Black Hat® conference, he highlighted how too many home routers have been compromised and are now making up a huge percentage of devices in botnets. We talk about the home component because a huge number of home workers continue to have a false sense of security from their misnamed devices. Can you really trust a VPN coming in from a compromised device? Even if you can trust the remote device, can you trust that the kid's computers aren't compromised? Are your trusted workers on the same network as their family's computers? We've long maintained that the barbarians are already inside the walls, and that perimeter security is dead. What should be happening is that the trusted worker should at the very least be in a separate zone so that the security device separates their machine from the rest of their family network. We also believe that you need to extend your view of corporate security out to the real edge of your network, the home worker. Stop using those low-cost devices and put in a security device that can actually do deep packet inspection and do real intrusion prevention.

Now let's flip the coin and talk about why real security appliances really can help. A well-designed security appliance starts off with an up-to-date and secured operating system. Linux isn't bad, just like Windows® or Mac® OS X® isn't bad. Real security appliances start off with a team just to make sure that the base operating system has had all its historical vulnerabilities removed, and under most circumstances the development team will most likely write new more secure modules to replace general-purpose modules such as web servers. True security appliances also tend to have some pretty aggressive testing done to them, and most times this is where the differences between devices arise. Just how aggressive the testing team is will pay dividends for the end users. During a big firewall test at *InfoWorld* magazine, Brian chose to run the entire CERT[1] collection of vulnerabilities against the outside of the firewall, the inside, and through a VPN. The intent was to simulate malware and attacks from the likely attack vectors and to confirm that these security devices were capable of finding and stopping all the known attacks to that date. The bottom line is that you get what you pay for, and the development costs for enterprise grade security devices include a massive amount of testing and fine-tuning.

Using Software to Manage Cloud Security

The issue here is that you don't always have the ability to insert a hardware appliance into your cloud vendor's infrastructure, especially if you're in a shared environment. However, what you can do is leverage the testing investment from security device vendors to insert virtual versions into your cloud. A good example is the SonicWall® SSL-VPN appliance that is also available as a virtual machine to provide a secure method to access your sensitive virtual networks or the Microsoft "DirectAccess" remote access system that integrates IPsec VPNs into an automated client system. Such a virtual appliance has become commonplace for most enterprise-grade security companies and leverages their testing investment for secure remote access. Additionally a common feature is the ability to authenticate against a directory-based source such as RADIUS, Active Directory®, or LDAP. This way a user expired in the directory system automatically has their remote access credentials removed as well.

The danger we've found involves an all too common underestimation of the complexity of some remote access systems such as the Citrix® NetScaler® gateway system. Brian's personal experience found that although NetScaler provides a huge array of authentication and remote access control, this advanced level of configuration too often is beyond the experience level of most IT shops, forcing you to purchase external help. In addition, keep in mind that although network specialists tend to thumb their nose at simplistic GUI systems, the hidden cost is that becoming proficient in the more complex command line isn't always cost effective for smaller shops. We tend to like a mixed approach that combines a guided GUI that allows for correct implementation of advanced features, with a command line once the GUI becomes too cumbersome.

Another all too common knee-jerk reaction is for IT shops to bridge remote access through a general-purpose operating system. This is typically implemented as an SSH connection into a Linux virtual machine that has a second network interface onto a secure network for management access. Although nothing is wrong with the concept, it requires that attention be paid to making sure that you take the extra effort to adequately secure that Linux machine. If said Linux machine has something like an SSH vulnerability, then an attacker can gain access to that machine and then bridge over to the corporate jewels. Do you have enough internal expertise to create a secure Linux implementation?

Test and Confirm Those Vendor Claims

Testing throughput and vulnerabilities in the cloud are topics almost never associated with clouds but really ought to be. Testing in general used to be commonplace in many larger IT organizations, but as bandwidth and network capabilities have exceeded most organizational needs, actively testing the network has fallen away. What hasn't been noticed is that complexity of this same network infrastructure has risen in response to a trend to combine more and more organizational functions onto what has traditionally been an IT-only resource, tipping the scales back in favor of oversubscription. Now, what we're seeing are latency and jitter sensitive functions like VoIP, video on demand, video conferencing, and storage area networks. With a new trend emerging to extend many of these services into the cloud, it might be a good idea to consider resurrecting that testing facility.

We'd like to remind folks again that this entire wonderful network infrastructure is driven by software, which is written by humans. Humans make mistakes that sometimes show up in some very creative ways. We can't even guess as to how many devices have failed spectacularly during testing, with some network devices even catching on fire. They all worked fine under "normal" loads, but have failed in some very creative ways when we've cranked it up to the vendor's advertised limits. One switch sounded like popcorn popping when we cranked it up and let out the magic blue smoke. At the advertised limits of the device, all the fiber optic control chips literally blew their tops and left craters across the entire collection. So although these are some extreme cases, some of the less extreme had some switches mangling multicast video packets, once we started streaming the equivalent of 100 1mb/sec video streams. Some switches lost the ability to prioritize traffic once we got the gigabit switch up over 50 percent utilization. We've also found some switches that started leaking traffic from the management port over to the production default VLAN once switch utilization got high enough. All symptoms that could have been exposed during a testing phase, but without testing, showed up on the production network at the worst possible time. We'd like to give kudos to folks like Ixia Communication and Spirent Communications who have spent an enormous amount of time and money developing equipment designed to test against industry standards for performance and functionality. The downside to these devices is the required skill level necessary to run these massively expensive devices, considering that each gigabit port on this type of test tool is capable of running millions of MAC addresses, and full line speed is a pretty good indication that this is some very special gear. So yes they fully deserve what they charge for them, but that doesn't mean that network testing is out of the range of smaller organizations. We're VERY fond of the Ixia Communications IxChariot® test tool that consists of a control console app (which is licensed) and free host services controlled by the console. What makes this oh so unique and wonderful is the ability to configure a mesh between any of the IxChariot Endpoints of synthetic traffic. So even if you're running an IxChariot Endpoint on a Raspberry Pi®, the synthetic traffic can be VoIP, IP Video, http, ftp, ssh, or any of hundreds of traffic profiles. The more powerful the endpoint, the more synthetic traffics streams that can be generated in a huge mesh. You can literally run a synthetic version of your entire organization after hours and push your infrastructure in a variable size "what if" to test if your infrastructure is capable of adding that new service.

What synthetic load testing also does is expose weaknesses in your infrastructure's capabilities by loading it up under controlled conditions. So it's better that it fails under testing rather than during a critical time period. For instance, quite a few VoIP controllers have a very finite amount of processor capability and, when pushed, can fail in many different ways. We've seen some fail open (i.e., make the connection even with invalid credentials) or fail closed (i.e., good credentials, but it took too long to authenticate and timed out) and many other combinations. If VoIP is a critical infrastructure piece, then running synthetic traffic loads can help you better predict if that move to a cloud-based VoIP controller is even going to be able to work. Brian has also been using the Maxwell®2 synthetic degradation tool from InterWorking Labs, where he can dial in latency, jitter, errors and many other degradations to simulate satellite links, long haul point to point, and other types of connections not normally easy to simulate in a lab environment. An interesting result is how badly some web-based authentication systems will perform over simulated satellite links that have worked just fine on premise. One of Brian's favorite simulations is how he used the Maxwell to simulate a VPN connection from Honolulu to Beijing that revealed a need for dramatically different sets of timeouts to be configured for this long haul link.

Stop Doing Work as Administrator

No matter how much you trust your staff, it really isn't a very good idea to have an obfuscated audit trail, which is exactly what you get when you have shared superuser credentials. Having a unique superuser account for special functions also means that you have log entries uniquely identifying which superuser did what and when. A very old trick is to put a massively complex password on the real administrator or root user account and seal it up in an envelope. Then store that envelope in a locked file cabinet or safe so that you can avoid what Brian calls the "bus" situation. There are just some things that can't be done unless you're the real administrator, and if a bus hits your key person, you're sunk. Better to only open that envelope up under those special conditions, and, for the rest, have an unambiguous audit trail for system changes. It's also a decent way to help protect your staff against finger-pointing by adding that one extra layer of audit trail. The same goes for *nix systems where you would login as a normal user and issue the "su" command to actually do administrator work. You can certainly "su" to your alternate superuser identity instead of the actual root user.

The Single Console: Security Management's Holy Grail

If you have the space and funding to build a network operations center, there is also a pretty good chance that you have several screens displaying product-specific dashboards or screens separating different functions from each other. What this also means is that your ability to correlate incidents across multiple systems is reduced to the point at which many organizations start suffering from a Silo Effect in their Network Operations Center (NOC).

While a single, all-encompassing monitoring system has some massive benefits for management and security, it also has a downside of probably being very complex. The University of Hawaii School of Ocean and Earth Science and Technology uses the ScienceLogic EM7™ carrier class monitoring system so that they can handle what isn't too different from a colocation facility. Their multitenant facility means that a single system is monitoring a huge number of variables, as well as providing a way to carve off research group–specific dashboards. So this compromise allows for thresholds to be set up for the entire organization, but daily monitoring responsibilities are delegated out to the individual research groups within the school.

We really don't have a good suggestion on a single, all-encompassing monitoring system. And, in reality, it's nearly impossible to integrate everything into a single system, short of a custom solution. It is, however, a good goal to minimize the number of systems through aggregation. The folks that design user interfaces measure display functionality by watching whether pupil movement is even or jerky. So you might consider sitting in front of the NOC denizens and watch their eye movements. Nice, even scanning means it's a more efficient display, and also has a great byproduct of reducing eye fatigue. Exactly what the designers at Boeing Aircraft wanted when they were designing the new glass cockpit for the 777 aircraft.

Summary

What this boils down to is that monitoring shouldn't be an afterthought as you plan any new system. Test it, confirm the vendor claims, make sure your infrastructure can handle your upgrade, and then take a good hard look at what you're monitoring, and ensure that the appropriate people are involved with monitoring. Perhaps as machine learning improves, you might start seeing it applied to monitoring systems, but until then, don't ignore the human factors.

References

1. "Computer Emergency Response Team." (2017). en.wikipedia.org. Accessed December 26, 2017, from https://en.wikipedia.org/wiki/Computer_emergency_response_team
2. "KMAX|IWL." (2017). iwl.com. Accessed December 26, 2017, from http://iwl.com/products/kmax

Chapter 20

Closing Comments

Here, the question is whether you should consider keeping all the management tools in house or whether you should consider delegating them to a cloud provider. We're imagining a balance, but if the provider is saying the right things, maybe the human resources (HR) cost savings are worth it if the provider is also willing to take responsibility for certain functions. Just keep in mind our section on service-level agreements (SLAs) and whether remediation benefits you or the provider.

Understand the Appliances and Systems Your Cloud Provider Can Control

What are the responsibilities, and are the remediation terms in your favor or the provider? It's certainly tempting to reduce your HR costs by shifting some of the management responsibilities to the provider, but can you live with the terms? Here, we ask, Have you defined a clear demarcation line so that responsibilities are unambiguous, and have you made this determination before you have an incident? A good example is how some private traffic camera companies have been found guilty of fudging tickets because they're profit driven and take a cut of every ticket issued, whereas a city employee might be more interested in what's best for the community. We'd also like to stress that continually updating the training of your personnel shouldn't be viewed as a money pit but rather an investment in personnel not making mistakes from lack of training.

It isn't so much which and what kind of appliances or facilities, but more along the line of balancing your costs and liabilities. If you've delegated the management of your private virtual networks to the provider and they unintentionally create an incident because they've accidentally bridged your private management network to the world; what are the provider's responsibilities? Here are some additional questions that you need to identify and things you need to do before you sign on the dotted line:

- What do change orders cost you?
- Who pays for mistakes in those change orders?
- Do you have a notification and approval method for changes driven by the provider?
- Have you defined remediation methods, both in terms of labor and loss of business?
- What are the termination terms and who owns the configurations?
- Are there fees and labor charges involved with moving your domain pieces?
- What kinds of procedures are there for changes to access that should include passwords, user accounts, access control lists, firewall rules, etc.?
- Take a hard look at anything that costs you money and/or time.
- Make sure you understand their methodology for defining access control lists (ACLs) and firewall rules. Don't assume bidirectionality.
- If authentication is via some sort of directory system, are you entitled to an export if you choose to sever ties? Is this an extra charge or part of the termination agreement?
- Who's responsible for documentation changes, especially things like as-built networks and logical diagrams of your system?
- At what point in your cloud system does the provider's responsibility end and yours start?

What we're trying to get at is that you can't take a completely hands-off approach. At the very least, you need to have trusted people to understand what the systems are capable of so that you don't accidentally ask for something impossible and have the provider burn up hundreds of billable hours chasing a red herring. We'd like to suggest that even if you don't have "experts" on staff, that your staff members at least be trained well enough to be able to tell if the provider is trying to pad their billable hours. Brian teaches his college students how to terminate fiber optics, not because he wants the kids to become fiber installers, but rather so they appreciate what goes into the systems, have the ability to write better bid specs and know when a vendor is trying to snow them.

Now, let's get to credentials. Are you sharing superusers, are they delegating, what are they delegating, do you get notification of access changes? Again, who, what, where, when, and how do you get access to your critical components, and who's responsible for each piece? Does your provider have some sort of change management system so that you can do self-service changes, or must a human be involved? Keep in mind that credentials aren't just usernames and passwords, but in many cases they should also involve certificates, public and private keys, and, in some cases, some sort of multifactor authentication (MFA) system. How do you handle biometrics if someone leaves your organization, and just what is the process of changing biometric access credentials for key personnel?

Conversations with Your Vendors: Understand How They Hook into APIs

Application programming interfaces (APIs) are a huge can of worms in that they provide you with access to your data, but in what is hopefully a well-supported method by your provider. If you're talking about a platform such as Amazon Web Services™ or Microsoft® Azure®, then there's a pretty good chance your provider has a large collection of "how-to" documents and/or videos on using the API. The point here is that a new API probably also includes a learning curve for your development staff, and it's important that your provider has methods to help your staff learn the finer points of using and securing those APIs.

Most important: What are your provider's policies on testing with a draft system so that you don't put your production data at risk? Does your provider offer a draft system? Or are you dependent upon virtual machine rollbacks? Too many systems people just take the word of the developers about load testing, only to find the application falling flat on its figurative face on its launch date by performing below the sales expectations. Using a real load tester is a wise investment, and testing should be done for every release, not just the major ones.

Who Is Allowed to Use Those APIs and Who Can Manage Them?

Just like a web browser interface, APIs need some sort of credential system for management. Does the provider's system use a security model to delegate credentials to the application or to users? Brian, for one, likes the model in which API credentials are actually dual-key encryption certificates, where the application is assigned the credential instead of a physical user. This way, development teams can decouple user-access credentials from API credentials.

What Connection Technologies Does the API Set Provide For?

Although certificates are great, having one connect through an encrypted transport gets past the "all your eggs in a single basket" scenario, which is all too typical in many mobile apps. What kinds of controls does the provider have to reduce the risks of unauthorized connections?

Where Are Connections Allowed From?

If the API is used for data access to the corporate database from a web portal, connections certainly shouldn't be allowed from the rest of the public Internet. Is there some sort of access control list that you can add to limit where connections are allowed? Who makes those changes?

When Are Connections Allowed?

Is this a 24×7 application or is this something that should only be available during working hours in each time zone? Are there methods to create exceptions for internal users working long hours? Who can make those changes?

How Does the Change Process Work?

If you've implemented the API connection to salesforce.com, then a connection from a stand-alone computer should immediately be suspect. Are changes done by you or the provider? Is this a change order?

Brian's Soapbox:

We'd like to emphasize one last major point: Your IT infrastructure is almost never a cookie cutter affair, and there is always some sort of customization involved. Treat your IT staff as frustrated artists that, given the opportunity, could very well put tools together in a truly artistic manner and turn your IT infrastructure into a work of art instead of just a box of knobs. Take the time and budget into every project time and resources to test before you turn the "customers" loose. We've both seen some truly massive projects go off the rails because the decision makers chose to believe the sales people and didn't make sure to test to see if the product really could fulfill the sales promises. Just like you wouldn't buy an expensive car without a test drive, take the system for a test drive WITH your data.

Curtis' Soapbox:

The days of human configuration of and intervention in cloud security processes—at least, as a routine way of making security happen—is rapidly coming to an end. The early cloud dreams of highly elastic and dynamic environments able to change and keep pace with the speed of modern business have come true. As a result, cloud application delivery systems are so complex, and change so rapidly, that humans can't effectively keep up. Security automation is quickly becoming the norm.

Of course, automation doesn't relieve security professionals of responsibility, or the requirement that they know what good cloud security looks like. Humans must still design and implement automated systems, and humans remain far superior to computers in analyzing novel and anomalous behaviors and conditions. Cloud security will be a hybrid of human and machine intelligence, in which machine intelligence deals with configuration and routine analysis while humans focus on design, analysis, and worst-case remediation.

Although speed remains the highest virtue in most business processes today, so many vulnerabilities and data-loss scenarios have been caused by simple misconfigurations and mistakes that it's worth taking the time to make a simple plea: Stop. Think. Think again. Then do. Build redundancy into processes that make significant changes to infrastructure and key process components. Don't be afraid to throw a little friction into a process if the result is significantly better security. And always argue in favor of more testing rather than less when it comes to approval steps for deployment.

New developments in machine learning, artificial intelligence (AI), and automation should make cloud security stronger and more reliable. That won't happen automatically, though, and it won't happen without human involvement.

Index